RECORDED VERSIONS
GUITAR®

AUTHENTIC TRANSCRIPTIONS
WITH NOTES AND TABLATURE

R&B GUITAR BIBLE

ISBN 978-0-634-02286-9

HAL•LEONARD®
CORPORATION

7777 W. BLUEMOUND RD. P.O. BOX 13819 MILWAUKEE, WI 53213

Visit Hal Leonard Online at
www.halleonard.com

Boogie Oogie Oogie

Words and Music by Janice Marie Johnson and Perry Kibble

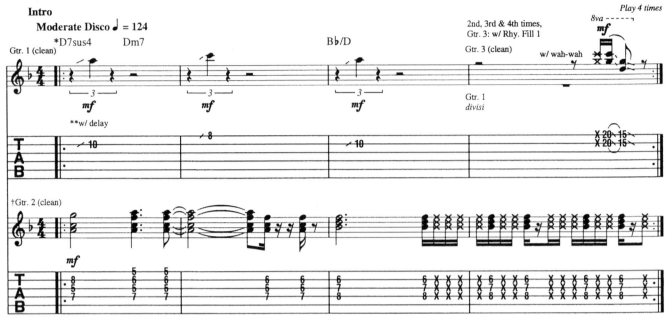

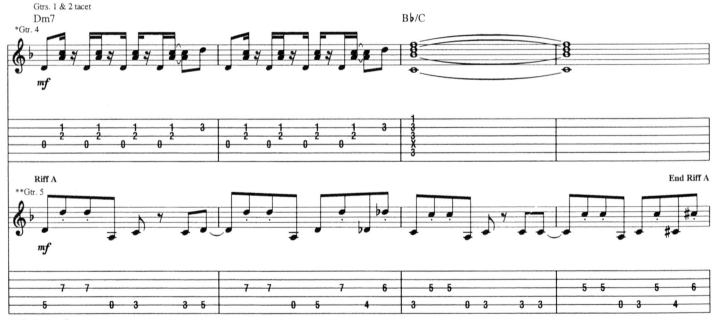

*Clarinet arr. for gtr.
**Bass arr. for gtr.

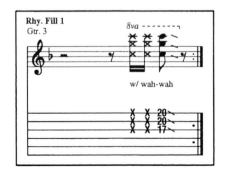

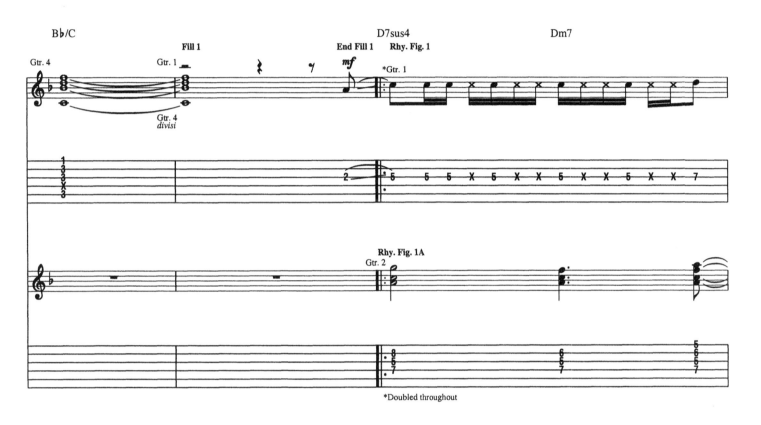

*Doubled throughout

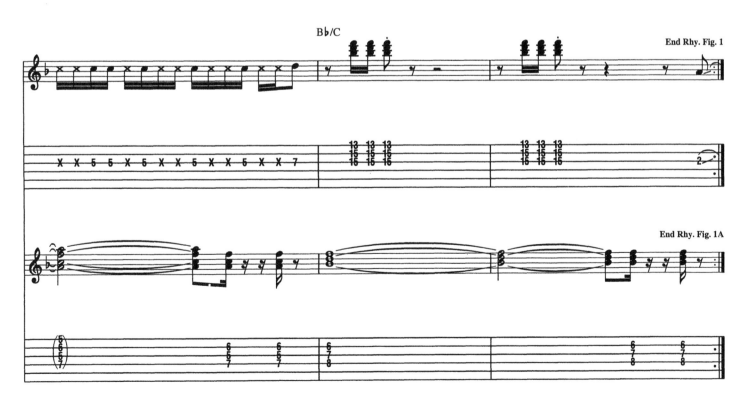

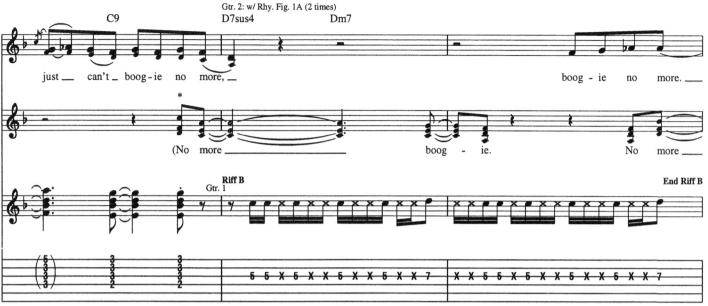

*Top notes of bkgd. voc. are sung by male voice and sound one octave lower than written.

Guitar Solo

Gtr. 1: w/ Rhy. Fig. 1 (3 3/4 times)
Gtr. 2: w/ Rhy. Fig. 1A (4 times)

Boog - ie!

Boom Boom (Out Go the Lights)

Words and Music by Stan Lewis

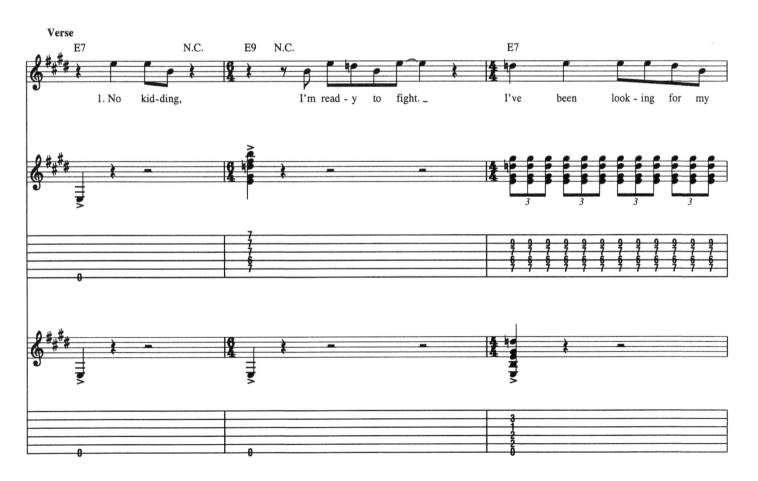

* Chord symbols reflect basic tonality.

ba - by all night. If I get her in my sight... Boom! Boom!

Out go the lights.

2. I thought I was treat-ing my ba - by fair, but now she's get-ting all in my hair. And

Gtr. 2: w/ Riff A

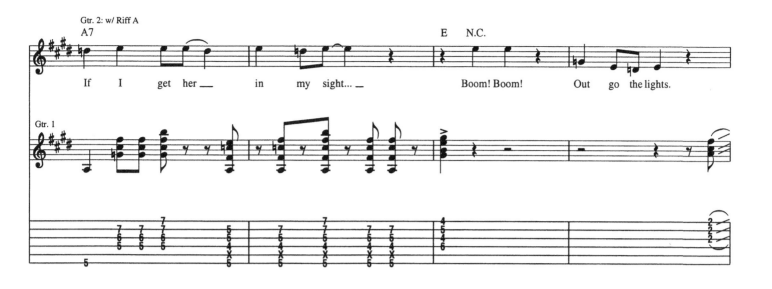

If I get her __ in my sight... __   Boom! Boom!   Out go the lights.

Outro-Harmonica Solo

Gtr. 2: w/ Riff B (1st 6 meas.)

Begin fade   *Fade out*

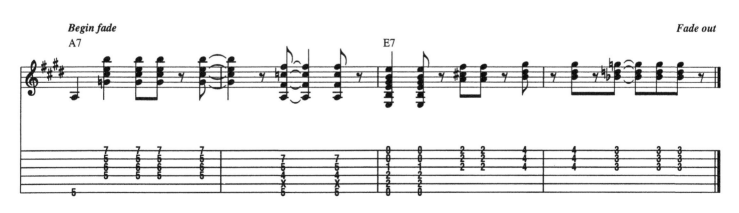

Brick House

**Words and Music by Lionel Richie, Ronald La Pread, Walter Orange,
Milan Williams, Thomas McClary and William King**

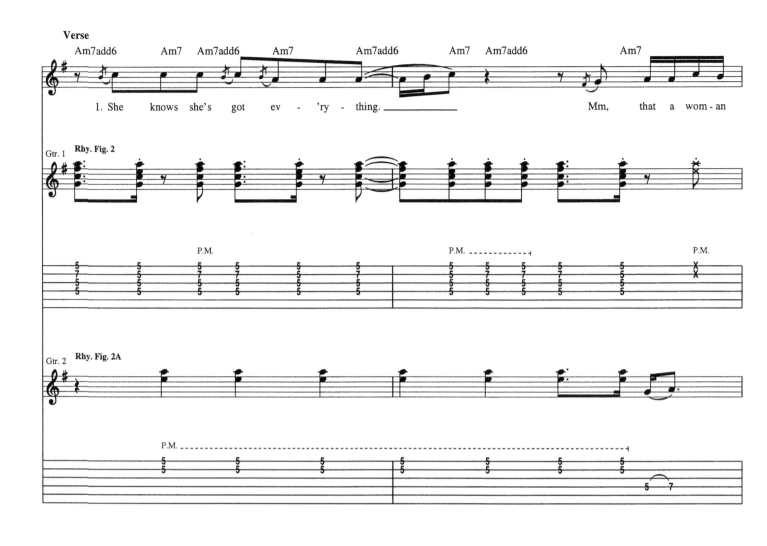

Verse

Am7add6   Am7 Am7add6   Am7   Am7add6   Am7 Am7add6   Am7

1. She knows she's got ev - 'ry - thing. _____ Mm, that a wom - an

Gtr. 1   **Rhy. Fig. 2**

Gtr. 2   **Rhy. Fig. 2A**

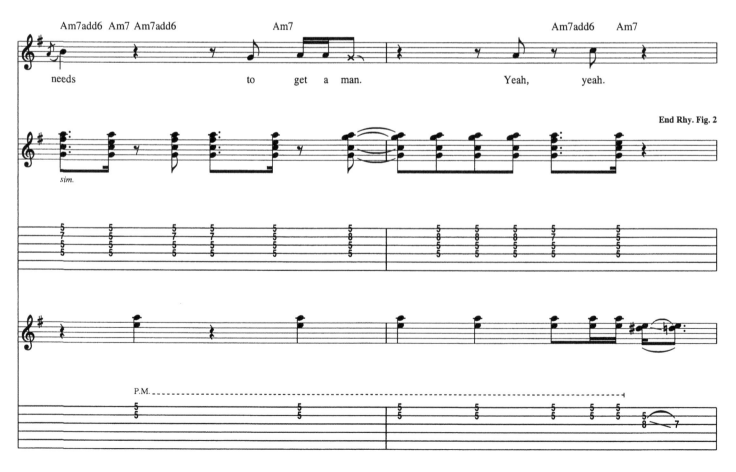

Am7add6 Am7 Am7add6   Am7   Am7add6   Am7

needs   to get a man.   Yeah,   yeah.

End Rhy. Fig. 2

sim.

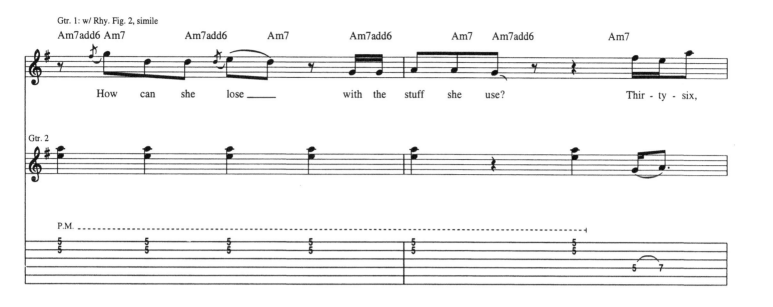

How can she lose ____ with the stuff she use? Thir-ty - six,

twen-ty-four, ____ thir-ty - six. Ow, what a win-ning hand - ful. She's a

Chorus

Gtr. 1: w/ Rhy. Fig. 1, 6 times, simile
Gtr. 2: w/ Rhy. Fig. 1A, simile

brick house. _ She's might-y, might - y ____ just let-tin' it all _ hang out. _ Ah, she's a

brick house. ____ Oh, ____ I like la - dies stacked _ and that's a fact. _

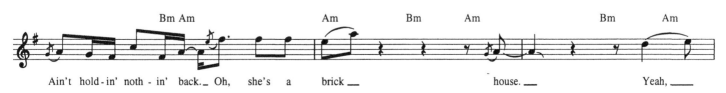

Ain't hold-in' noth - in' back. _ Oh, she's a brick ____ house. ____ Yeah, ____

19

Interlude

Gtr. 1 tacet

Am
(elec. piano)

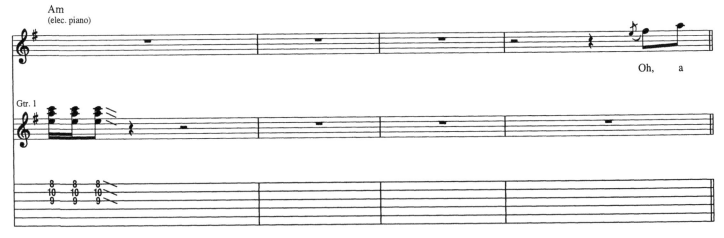

Oh,   a

Outro

N.C.

brick   house. ___

Gtr. 2

Begin Fade

*Chord symbols reflect implied tonality.

Fade Out

But It's Alright

Words and Music by Jerome L. Jackson and Pierre Tubbs

Xylophone Solo

Gtr. 1: w/ Rhy. Fig. 1, 4 times, simile
Gtr. 2: w/ Rhy. Fig. 1A, 4 times, simile

*Xylophone arr. for gtr.

Gtr. 1: w/ Rhy. Fig. 2, simile
Gtr. 2: w/ Rhy. Fig. 2A, simile
Gtr. 3 tacet

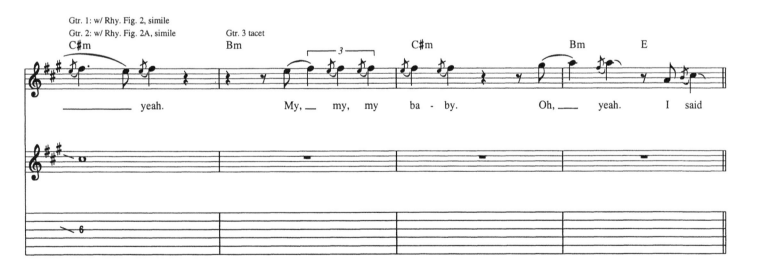

Chorus

Gtr. 1: w/ Rhy. Fig. 1, simile
Gtr. 2: w/ Rhy. Fig. 1A, simile

25

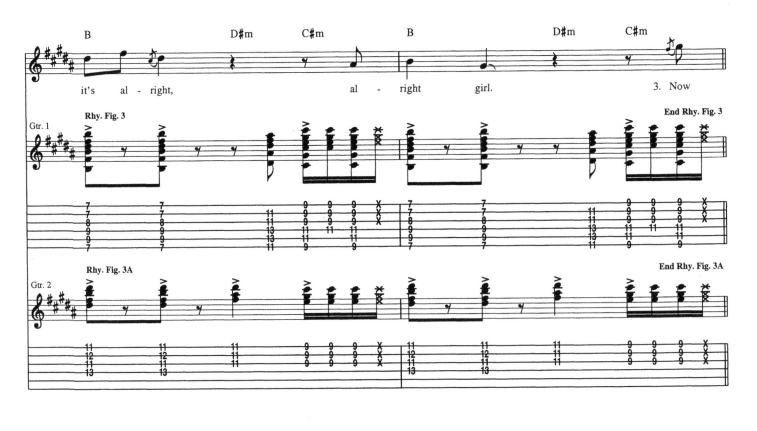

B   D#m   C#m   B   D#m   C#m

it's al - right,   al - right girl.   3. Now

Verse

Gtr. 1: w/ Rhy. Fig. 3, 4 times, simile
Gtr. 2: w/ Rhy. Fig.3A, 4 times, simile

there's one thing ___ I wan-na say. _____ You'll meet a guy who'll make you pay.   He'll

treat ya bad, ___ he'll make you sad and you will ru - in ___ the love you had. Oh, but I

hate _____ to say I told you so, ___ but,

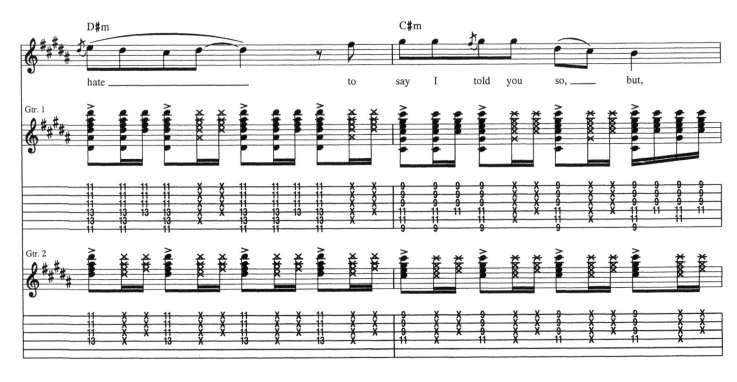

baby, you got to, got to reap _ what you sow, ____ girl. But

Chorus

Gtr. 1: w/ Rhy. Fig. 3, 2 times, simile
Gtr. 2: w/ Rhy. Fig. 3A, 2 times, simile

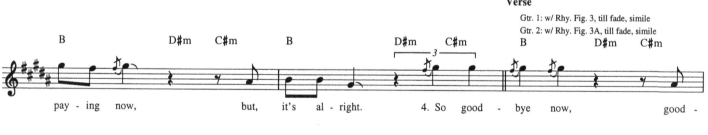

it's al - right, al - right, girl. You are

Verse

Gtr. 1: w/ Rhy. Fig. 3, till fade, simile
Gtr. 2: w/ Rhy. Fig. 3A, till fade, simile

pay - ing now, but, it's al - right. 4. So good - bye now, good -

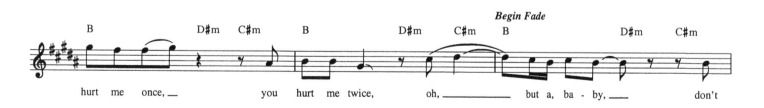

bye, girl. You're pay - ing now, so, bye - bye. You

Begin Fade

hurt me once, ___ you hurt me twice, oh, _____ but a, ba - by, ___ don't

Fade Out

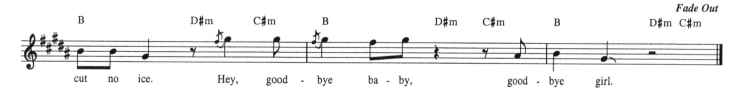

cut no ice. Hey, good - bye ba - by, good - bye girl.

Dancing in the Street

from GOOD MORNING VIETNAM

Words and Music by Marvin Gaye, Ivy Hunter and William Stevenson

29

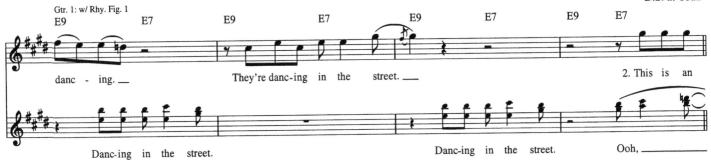

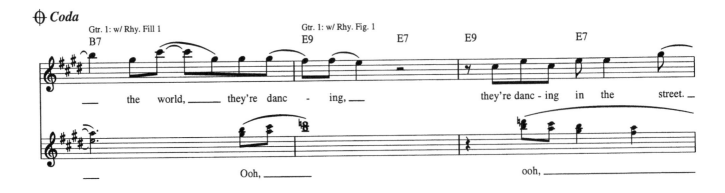

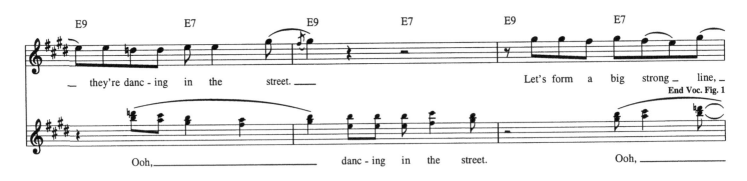

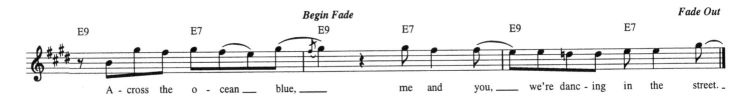

Fire

Words and Music by Ralph Middlebrooks, Marshall Jones, Leroy Bonner,
Clarence Satchell, Willie Beck and Marvin Pierce

* Chord symbols reflect basic harmony.

** Horns arr. for gtr.

Get Up (I Feel Like Being) a Sex Machine

By James Brown, Bobby Byrd and Ronald Lenhoff

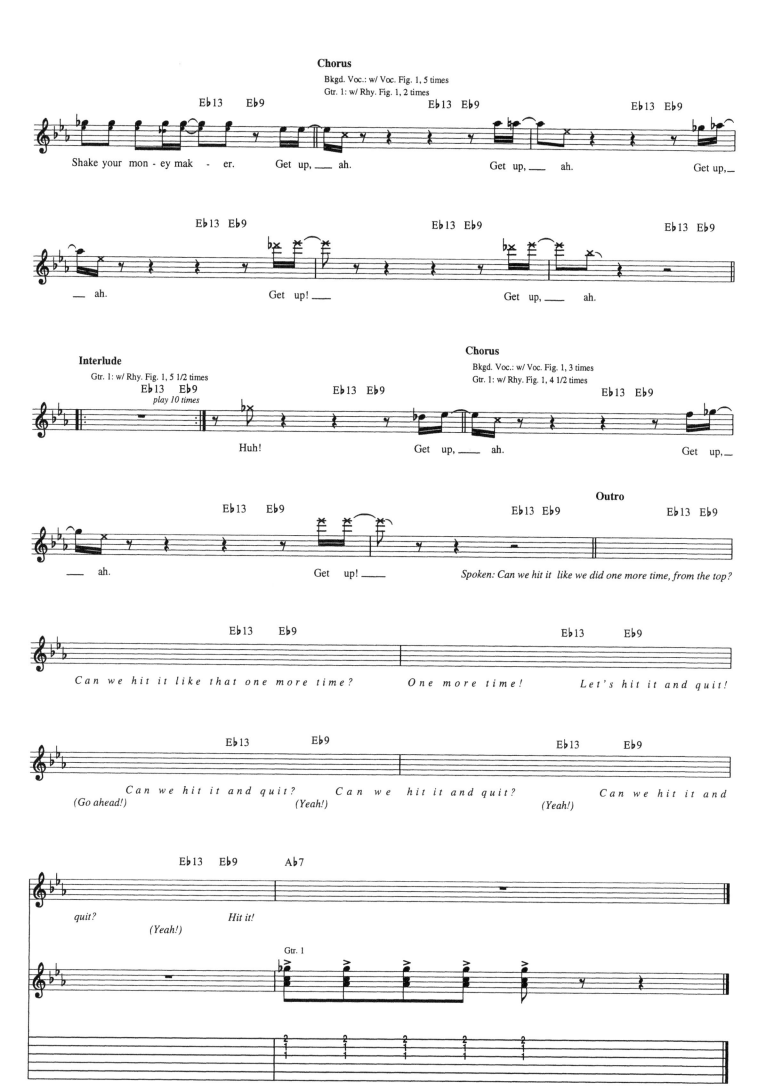

I Can't Help Myself
(Sugar Pie, Honey Bunch)

Words and Music by Brian Holland, Lamont Dozier and Edward Holland

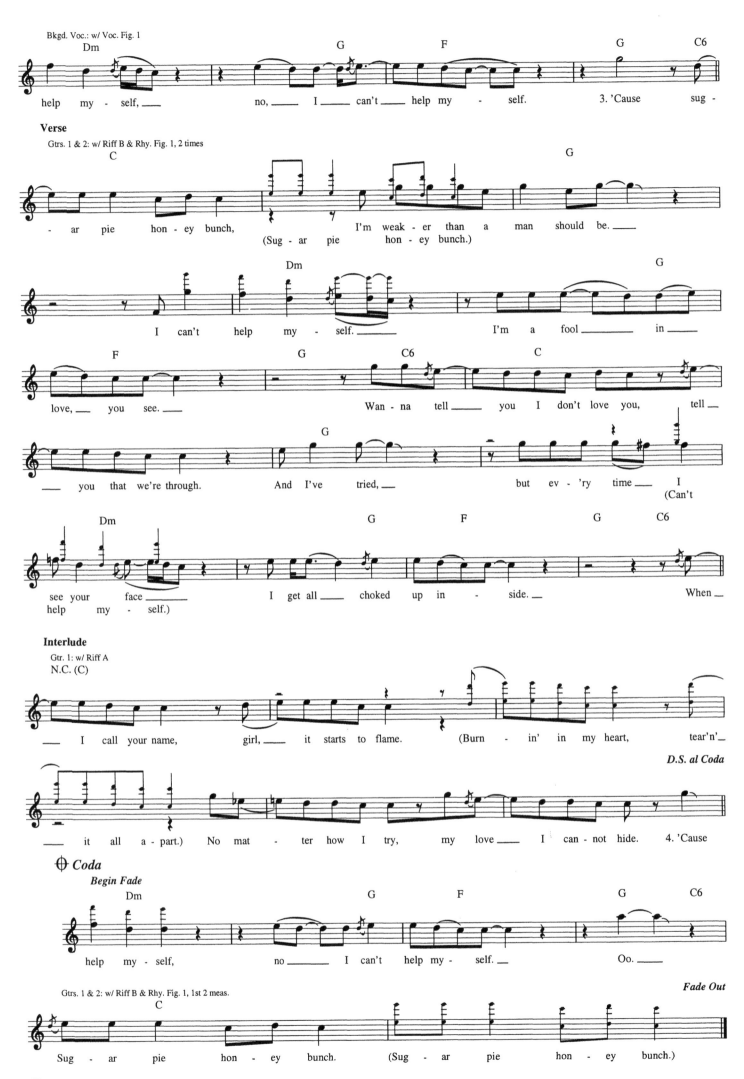

I Got the Feelin'

Words and Music by James Brown

Chorus

Gtr. 1: w/ Rhy. Fig. 1, 2 times
Gtr. 2: w/ Rhy. Fig. 2, 1 1/2 times

Gtr. 2: w/ Rhy. Fill 1

F7

Good God!   I _____ got the feel-in', uh.   Al - right.
Ba - by!   I got the feel-in', ba - by, can't help it.

Gtr. 2 tacet   C7   Gtr. 1 tacet

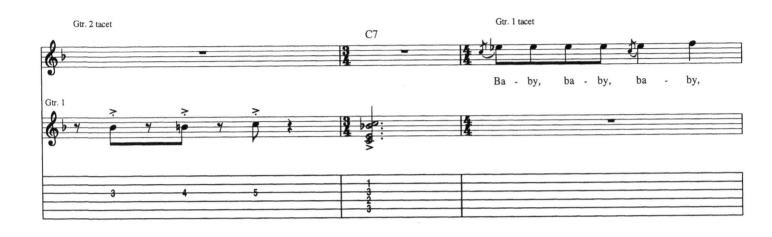

Ba - by, ba - by, ba - by,

Gtr. 1

To Coda ⊕

ba - by, ba - by, ba - by,   ba - by, ba - by, ba - by,   ba - by, ba - by.   2. I got the
                                                                                     I'm on a

Verse

Gtr. 1: w/ Rhy. Fig. 1, 7 times
Gtr. 2: w/ Rhy. Fig. 2, 7 times

F7

feel - in', ba - by.   Ba - by.

Some - times I'm up,   some - times I'm down. _____   My

heart, _____   al - right, _____ I'm a, real - ly down, _____ a lev - el with

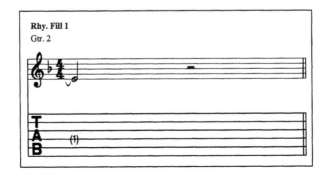

Rhy. Fill 1
Gtr. 2

the ground.   Ba -   by.   I   said   lev - el   with

Gtr. 1: w/ Rhy. Fig. 3
Gtr. 2 tacet
B♭7

the   ground. _   Whoa. _____   Ba -

- by, _____   you   treat   me,   treat   me.   bad.   Oh, ___

Interlude

D.S al Coda

Gtr. 1: w/ Rhy. Fig. 1, 2 times
Gtr. 2: w/ Rhy. Fig. 2, 2 times
F7

I   know,   I   know,   know   you   don't   mean   it   now. _   3. Some - times   I

⊕ *Coda*

Sax Solo

Gtr. 1: w/ Rhy. Fig. 1, till fade
w/ Vocal ad lib., till fade

Gtr. 2   F7

Begin Fade

Fade Out

I Got You
(I Feel Good)

Words and Music by James Brown

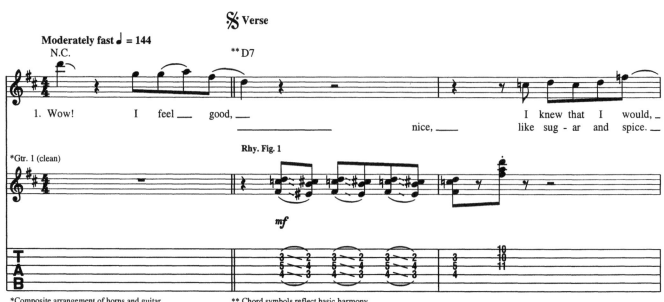

*Composite arrangement of horns and guitar.   ** Chord symbols reflect basic harmony.

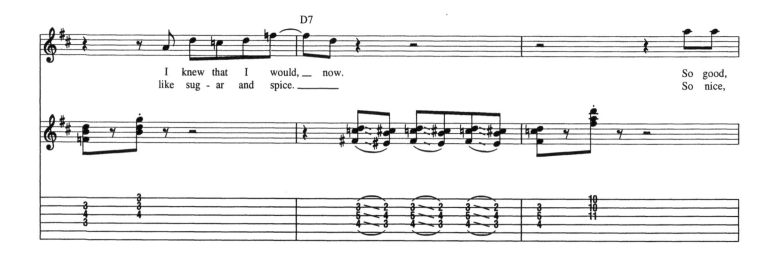

I Heard It Through the Grapevine

Words and Music by Norman J. Whitfield and Barrett Strong

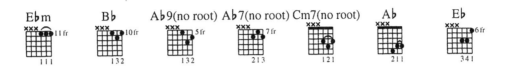

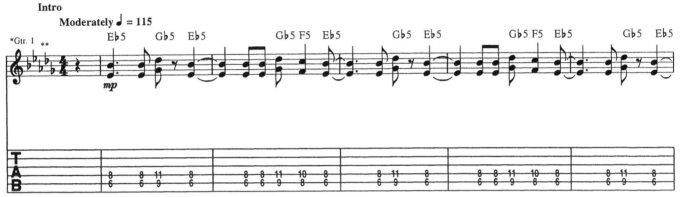

*Kybd. arr. for gtr.

**Key Signature denotes Eb Dorian

% Verse

54

⊕ *Coda*
Outro

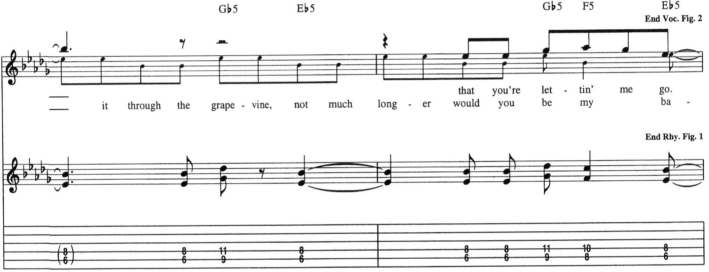

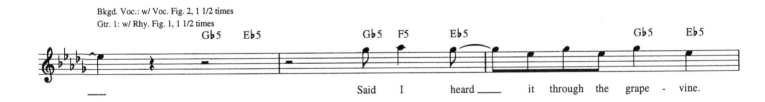

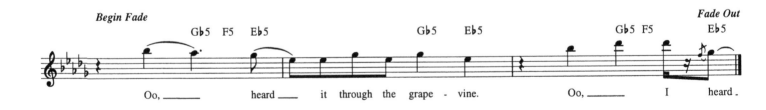

Additional Lyrics

2. I know a man ain't supposed to cry,
   But these tears, I can't hold inside.
   Losing you would end my life, you see.
   'Cause you mean that much to me.
   You could've told me yourself that you love someone else.
   Instead, I heard...

3. People say believe half of what you see.
   Some and none of what you hear.
   But I can't help from being confused.
   If it's true, please tell me dear.
   Do you plan to let me go for the other guy you loved before?

I Just Want to Celebrate

Words and Music by Nick Zesses and Dino Fekaris

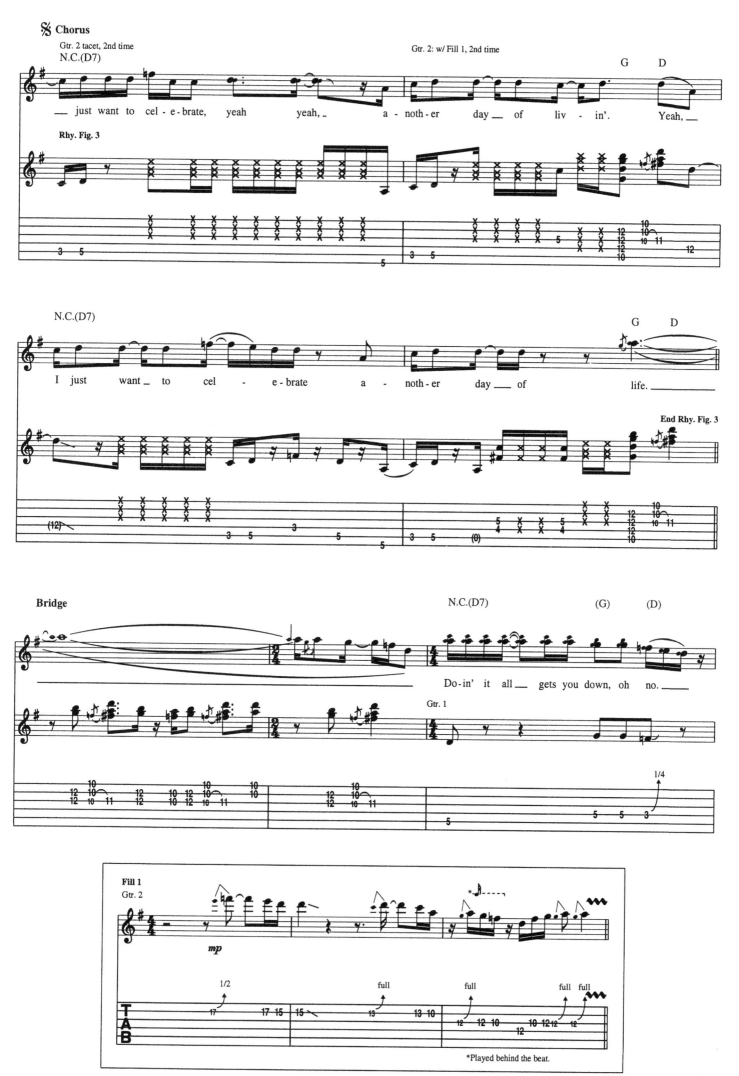

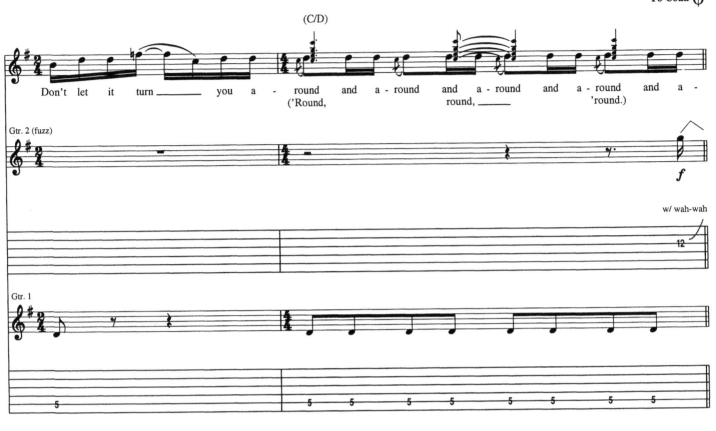

Don't let it turn _____ you a - round and a - round and a - round and a - round and a -
('Round, round, _____ 'round.)

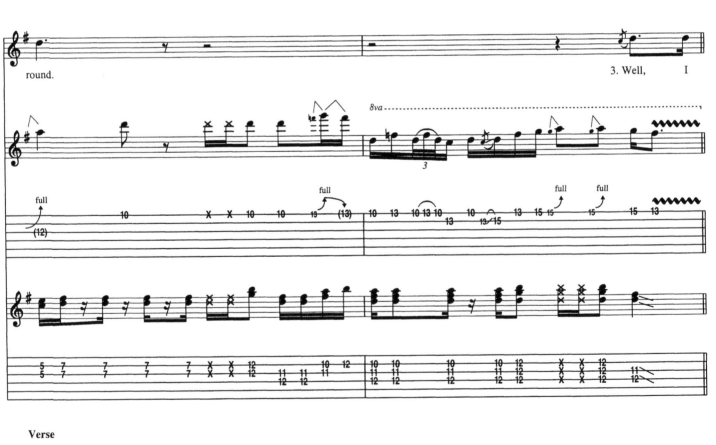

round.

3. Well, I

Verse

Gtr. 2 tacet
Gtr. 1: w/ Rhy. Fig. 2, simile

N.C.(D7)   G   D   N.C.(D7)   G   D

can't be both - ered with sor - row   and I   can't _ be both - ered with hate, _ no no.   I'm

I Second That Emotion

Words and Music by William "Smokey" Robinson and Alfred Cleveland

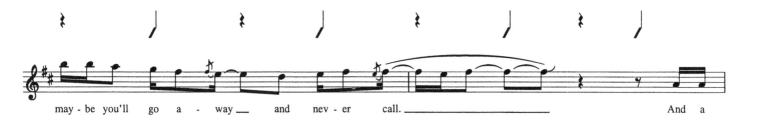

may - be you'll go a - way __ and nev - er call. _____ And a

Bridge

taste of ho-ney's worse __ than none at all. _____ Oh, __ lit-tle girl, in that case I don't want no part. __

_____ I do be - lieve that that would on - ly break my heart. _____ Oh, ____ but

Chorus

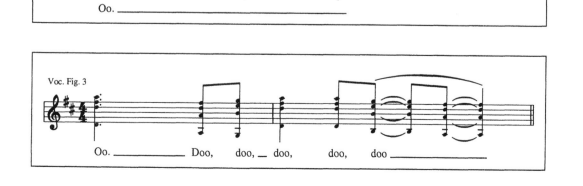

Or may-be you think that love ___ were made for fools. ___ And

so it makes ___ you wise ___ to break the rules. ___ Oh, ___ lit-tle girl then

Bridge

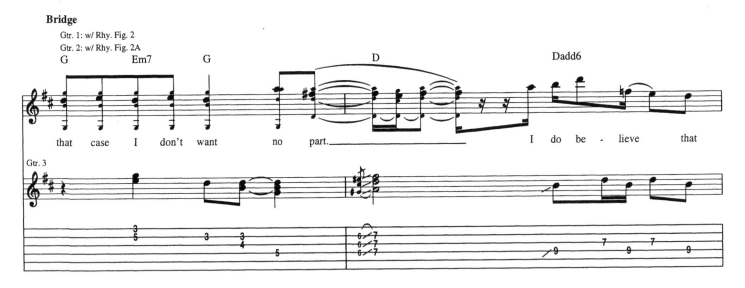

that case I don't want no part. ___ I do be-lieve that

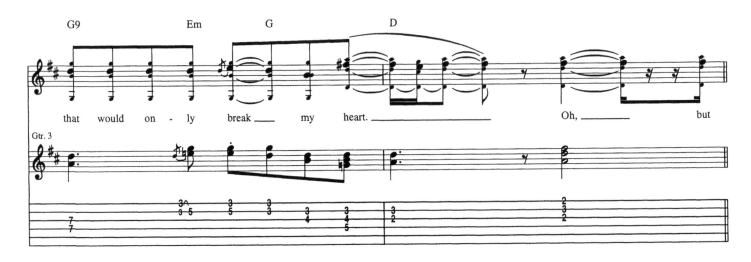

that would on-ly break ___ my heart. ___ Oh, ___ but

Chorus

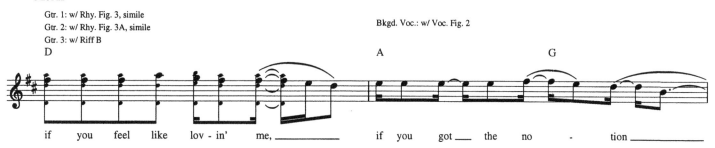

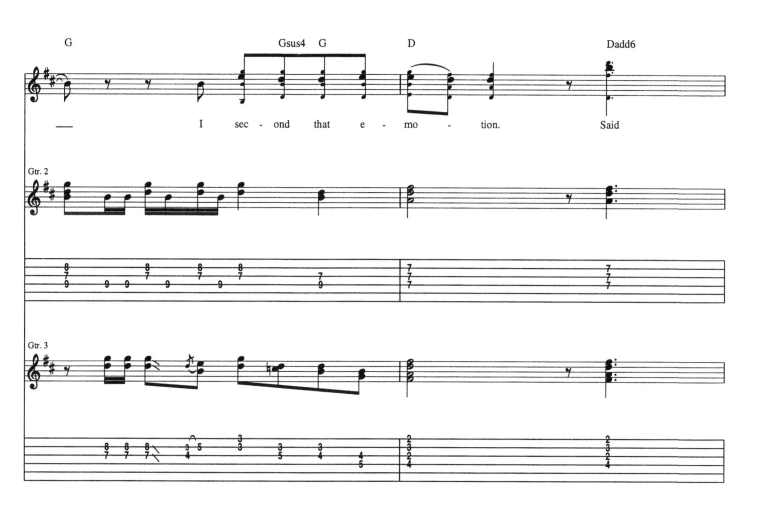

— uh,   I sec - ond that e - mo - tion.   Oh,   oh.

Interlude

Oh,   oh.

let ring

Bridge

Gtr. 1: w/ Rhy. Fig. 2
Gtr. 2: w/ Rhy. Fig. 2A

that case I don't want no part. ____ I do be - lieve ____ that

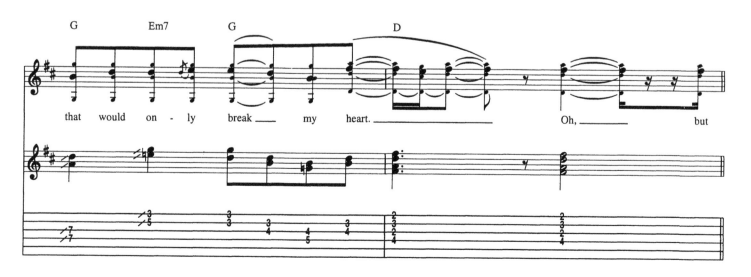

that would on - ly break ____ my heart. ____ Oh, ____ but

Chorus

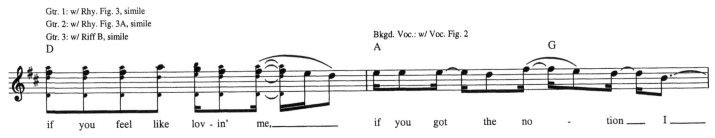

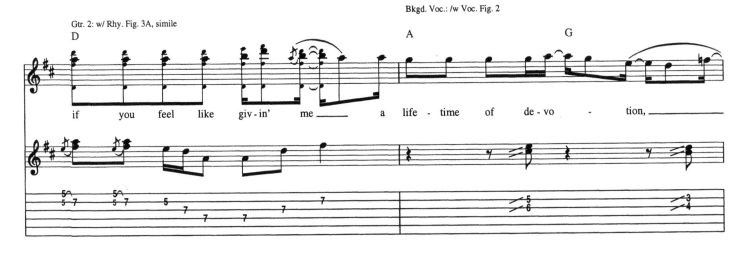

lit - tle girl, I sec - ond that e - mo - tion. Oo, ____

Begin Fade   *Fade Out*

____ lit - tle girl, I sec - ond that e - mo - tion.

I Wish

Words and Music by Stevie Wonder

Coda

er ____ have _ to _ go?   Ooh,   hoo.

Outro

Play 8 Times and Fade

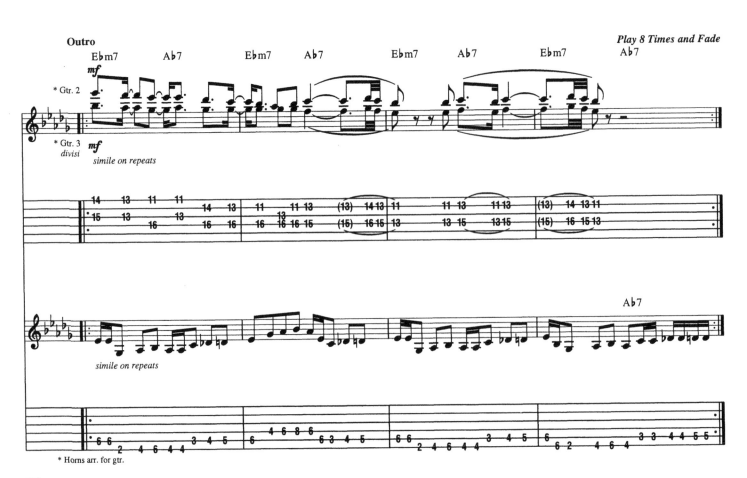

* Horns arr. for gtr.

76

It's Your Thing

By Rudolph Isley, Ronald Isley and O'Kelly Isley

Love Rollercoaster

Words and Music by Ralph Middlebrooks, James Williams, Marshall Jones,
Leroy Bonner, Clarence Satchell, Willie Beck and Marvin R. Pierce

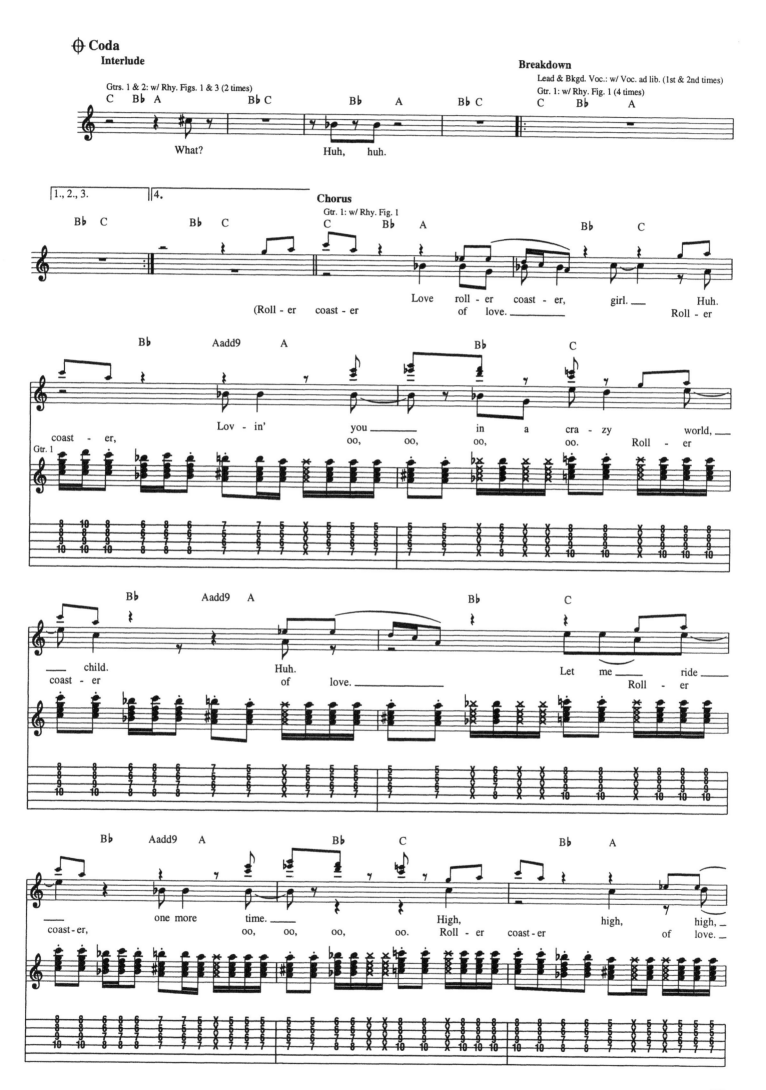

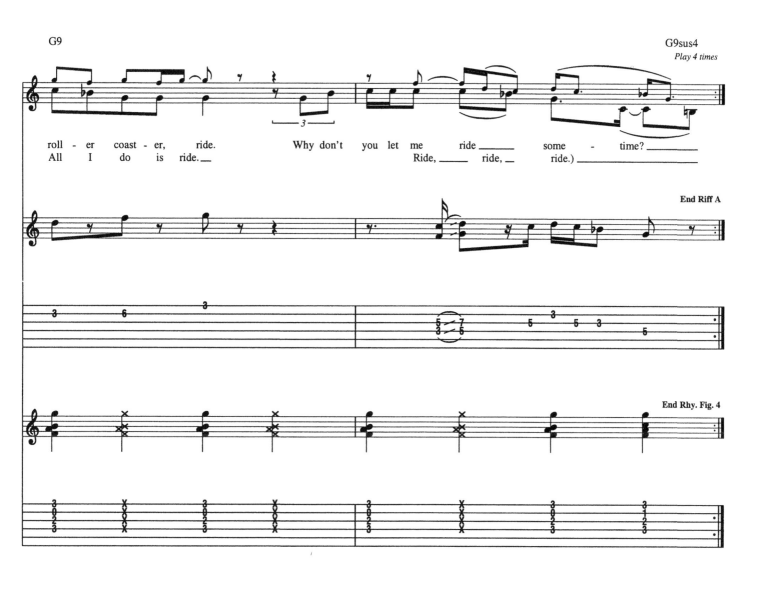

roll - er coast - er, ride. Why don't you let me ride _____ some - time? _____
All I do is ride. _____ Ride, _____ ride, _ ride.) _____

Lead Voc.: w/ Voc. ad lib. (till fade)
Gtr. 1: w/ Rhy. Fig. 4 (till fade)
Gtr. 2 tacet

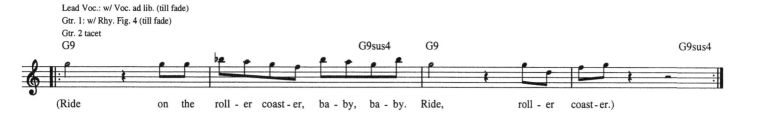

(Ride on the roll - er coast - er, ba - by, ba - by. Ride, roll - er coast - er.)

(Ride on the roll - er coast - er, ba - by, ba - by. Ride, roll - er coast - er.) _____

Gtr. 2: w/ Riff A (till fade)

(Ride on the roll - er coast - er, ba - by, ba - by. Ride, roll - er coast - er.) _____

Mustang Sally

Words and Music by Bonny Rice

*Chord in parenthesis is for Gtr. 4

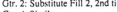

Gtr. 1: w/ Fill 12, 2nd time
Gtr. 2: Substitute Fill 2, 2nd time
Gtr. 4 Simile

Gtr. 1: w/ Fill 12, 2nd time

slow your Mus-tang down.
Now you're go-in' a-round sig-ni-fy-in' wom-an, you don't wan-na let me ride.

Gtr. 2

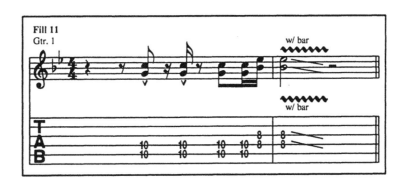

Fill 11
Gtr. 1

Fill 2
Gtr. 2

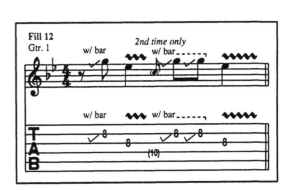

Fill 12
Gtr. 1

2nd time only

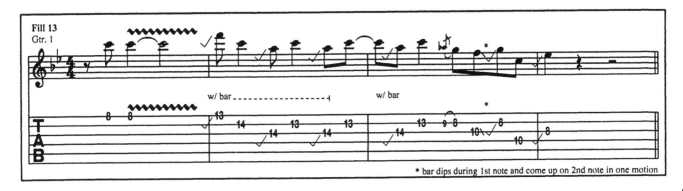

Fill 13
Gtr. 1

* bar dips during 1st note and come up on 2nd note in one motion

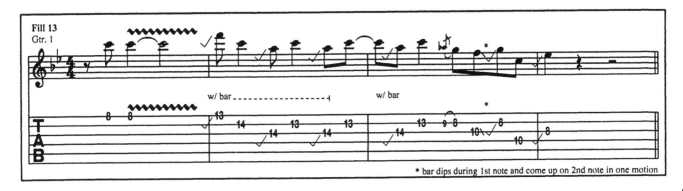

Gtr. 1: w/ Fill 13, 2nd time

Gtr. 2: Substitute Fill 3, 2nd time

F7(F5)

Mus-tang   Sal-ly,   ba - by,   I guess you bet-ter

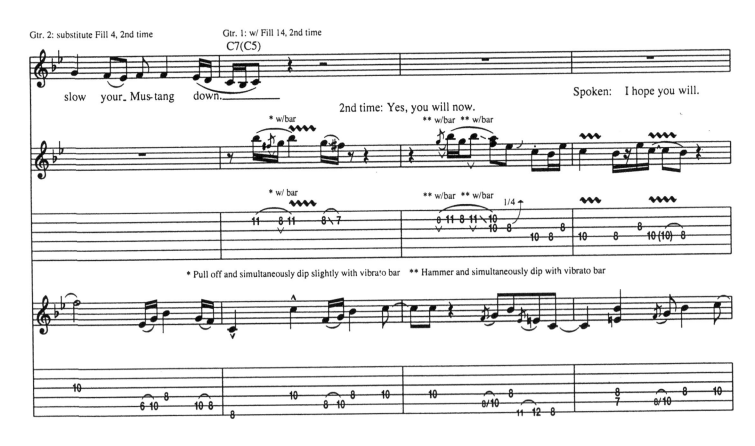

Gtr. 2: substitute Fill 4, 2nd time

Gtr. 1: w/ Fill 14, 2nd time

C7(C5)

slow   your Mus-tang   down.

2nd time: Yes, you will now.

Spoken: I hope you will.

* Pull off and simultaneously dip slightly with vibrato bar   ** Hammer and simultaneously dip with vibrato bar

Fill 3
Gtr. 2

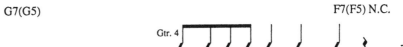

You bet - ter run it all ___ o - ver town. ___

Gon - na run all o - ver town. ___

I guess I bet - ter

I'm gon - na put your

All you wan-na do is ride___ a-round Sal - ly.___

(Ride Sal-ly, ride.)

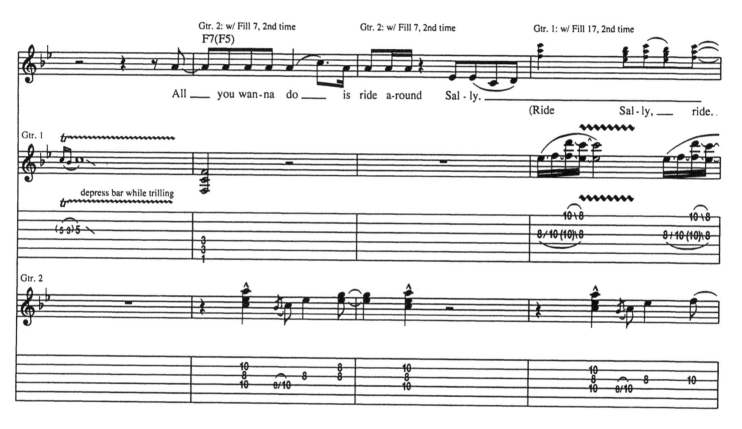

Gtr. 2: w/ Fill 7, 2nd time   Gtr. 2: w/ Fill 7, 2nd time   Gtr. 1: w/ Fill 17, 2nd time

F7(F5)

All ___ you wan-na do ___ is ride a-round Sal - ly. ___

(Ride Sal-ly, ___ ride. .

depress bar while trilling

Gtr. 1

Gtr. 2

Fill 6
Gtr. 2

Fill 16   w/ bar
Gtr. 1   w/ bar   w/ bar

w/ bar   w/ bar   w/ bar

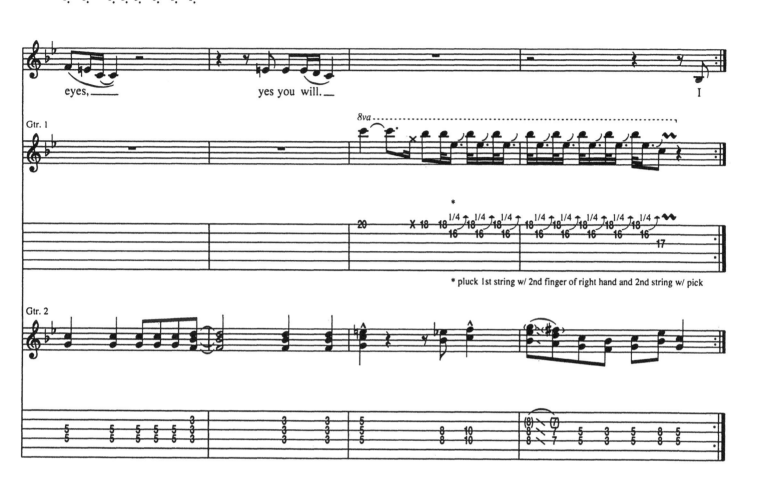

* pluck 1st string w/ 2nd finger of right hand and 2nd string w/ pick

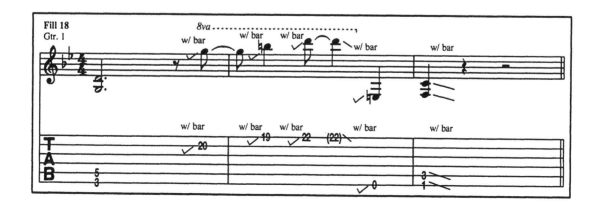

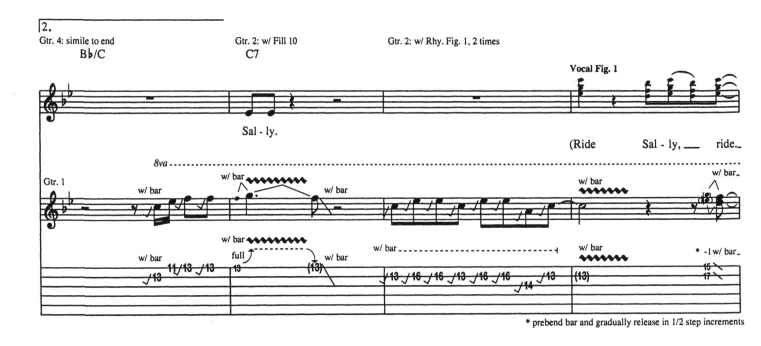

* prebend bar and gradually release in 1/2 step increments

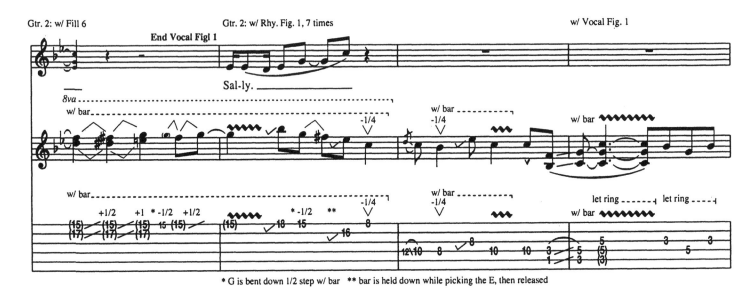

* G is bent down 1/2 step w/ bar ** bar is held down while picking the E, then released

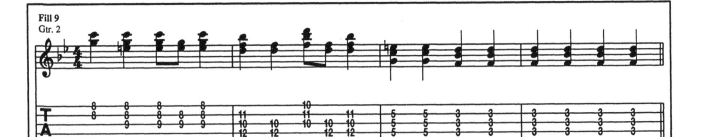

* depress bar while trilling

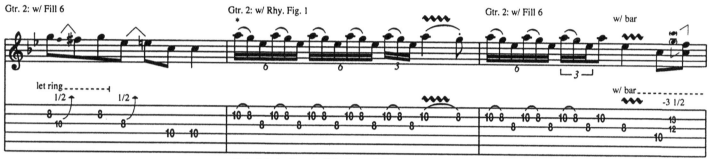

Gtr. 2: w/ Fill 6

Gtr. 2: w/ Rhy. Fig. 1

Gtr. 2: w/ Fill 6

* pluck 2nd string w/ middle finger of right hand, pulloff, and pluck 3rd string w/ pick

w/ Vocal Fig. 1
Gtr. 2: w/ Rhy. Fig. 1

Gtr. 2: w/ Fill 6

Gtr. 2: w/ Rhy. Fig. 1, 3 times

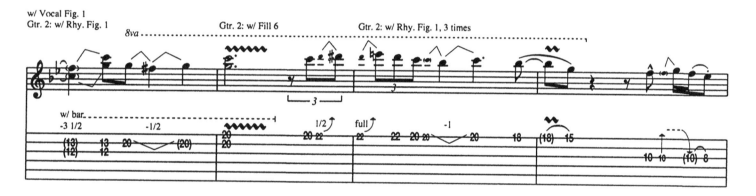

w/ Vocal Fig. 1

Gtr. 2: w/ Fill 6

Gtr. 2: w/ Rhy. Fig. 1, 4 times

pitch: F

Fade

My Babe

Written by Willie Dixon

* Chord symbols reflect basic harmony.

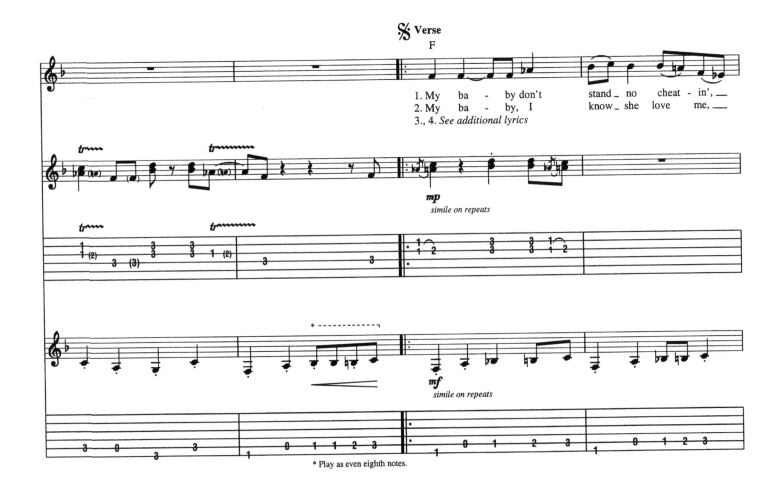

* Play as even eighth notes.

don't __ stand __ none o' that mid - night creep - in'. _____ My babe, true __
don't __ do ____ nut - tin' but kiss an' hug __ me. My babe, true __

4th time, to Coda ⊕

3rd time, Gtr. 1: w/ Fill 1

1.   2.

__ lit - tle ba - by, __ mm, my babe.
__ lit - tle ba - by, __ mm, my babe.

*Played as even
eighth notes.

Fill 1
Gtr. 1

She's my ba - by. True __ lit - tle ba - by. She's my ba - by. True __ lit - tle ba - by.

Additional Lyrics

3. My baby don't stand no cheatin', my babe.
   Oh no, she don't stand no cheatin', my baby.
   Oh no, she don't stand no cheatin',
   Ev'rything she do, she do so pleasin'.
   My babe, true little baby, my babe.

4. My baby don't stand no foolin', my babe.
   Oh yeah, she don't stand no foolin', my baby.
   Oh yeah, she don't stand no foolin',
   When she's hot, there ain't no coolin'.
   My babe, true little baby, she's my baby.
   True little baby.

My Girl

Words and Music by William "Smokey" Robinson and Ronald White

Chorus

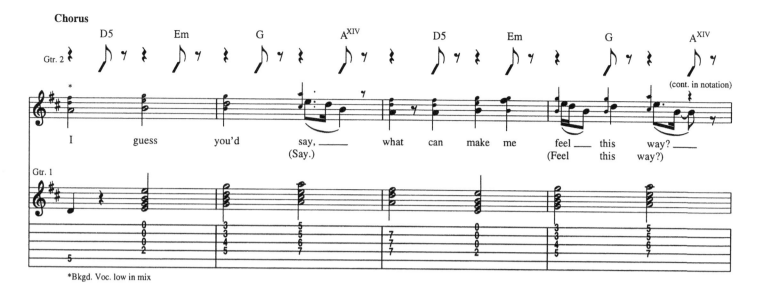

*Bkgd. Voc. low in mix

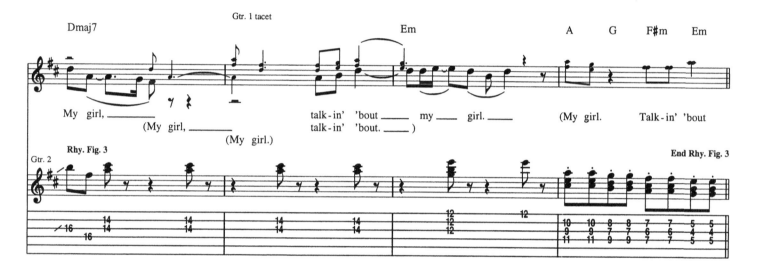

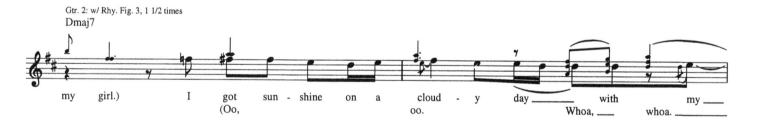

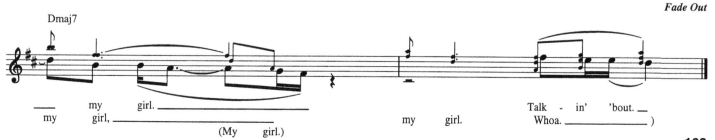

Nadine (Is It You)

Words and Music by Chuck Berry

you got some-thing else to do. ___
you're up to some - thing new. ___
you're up to some - thing new. ___

2. I

Outro
Gtr. 1: w/ Rhy. Fig. 1 (3 times)
Gtr. 2: w/ Riff A

Begin fade

Gtr. 1: w/ Rhy. Fig. 2

Fade out

Additional Lyrics

3. Downtown searching for her, looking all around.
   Saw her getting in a yellow cab, heading uptown.
   I caught a loaded taxi, paid up everybody's tab.
   Flipped a twenty dollar bill and told them, "Catch that Yellow cab."

4. She moves around like a wayward summer breeze.
   Go, driver. Go, go catch her for me please.
   Moving through the traffic like a mounted cavalier.
   Leaning out the taxi window trying to make her hear.

No Particular Place to Go

Words and Music by Chuck Berry

*Chord symbols reflect implied tonality.

I stole a kiss at the turn of a mile.
The night was young and the moon __ was gold,

My cu - ri - os - i - ty run-nin' wild. __
so we both de - cid-ed to take a stroll. __

Cruis - in' and play-in' the ra - di - o
Can you i - mag-ine the way __ I felt?

ear.

Cud - dl - in' more and driv - in' slow
Cruis - in' and play - in' the ra - di - o

To Coda ⊕

with no par - tic - u - lar place to go.
with no par - tic - u - lar place to

Guitar Solo

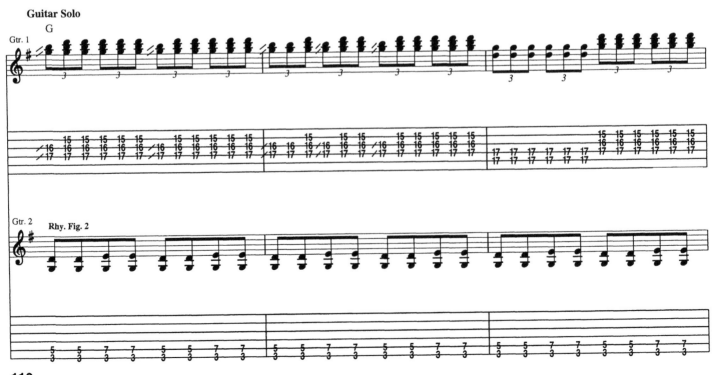

Gtr. 1

Gtr. 2 **Rhy. Fig. 2**

D.S. al Coda

3. No par - tic - u - lar place to

End Rhy. Fig. 2

⊕ *Coda*

Outro-Guitar Solo

Gtr. 2 w/ Rhy. Fig. 2

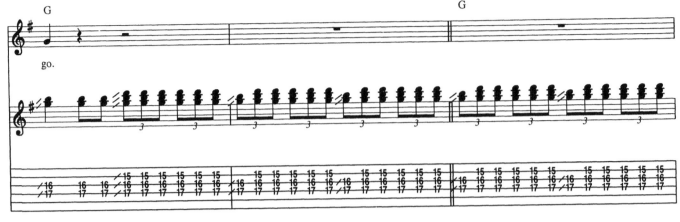

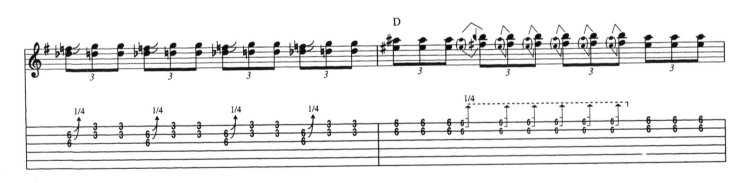

Pain in My Heart

Words and Music by Naomi Neville

Intro

* Horns arr. for gtr.
** Chord symbols reflect overall harmony.

Verse

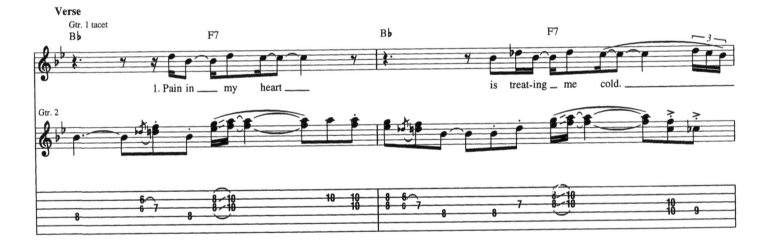

Verse

2. Pain in __ my heart __ just won't let me sleep. __

Where can __ my ba - by be? ___ Lord, __ where can she be? ___

𝄋 **Bridge**

2nd time, Gtr. 1 tacet
2nd time, Gtr. 2: w/ Fill 1

And now the days __ has be - gin to get { tough. __ / rough. __ } Said, I want you to

Fill 1
Gtr. 2

come back,   come back,   come_ back,   ba - by. ___   I had e - nough, _   oh. ___
love me,   love me,   love _ me,   ba - by, ___   till I get e - nough, _   oh. ___

Verse

3. A lit-tle pain in _ my heart ___ just won't let me be. ___

Wake up a-rest-less nights, _   Lord, _ and I can't e-ven sleep. _

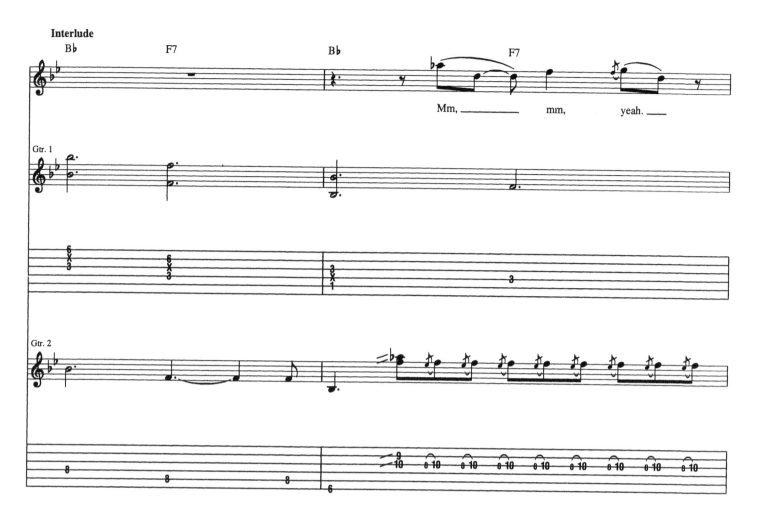

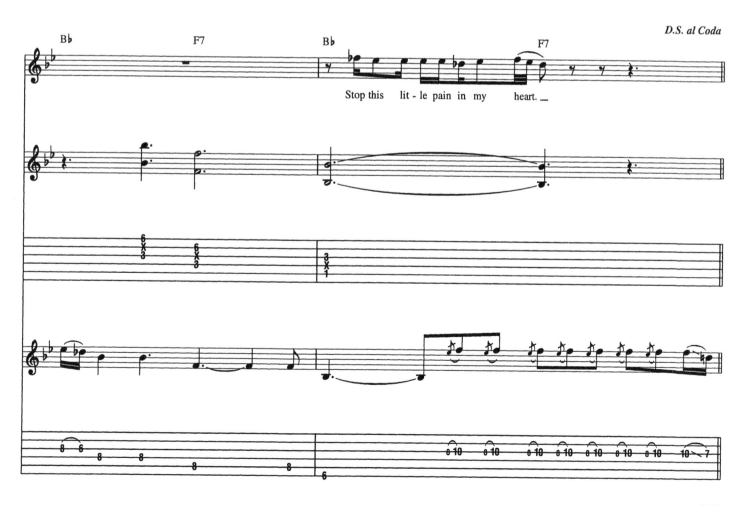

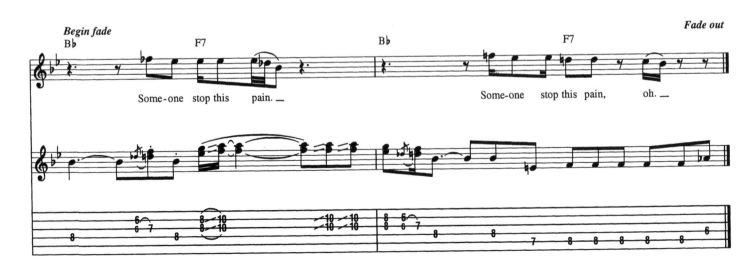

Papa Was a Rollin' Stone

Words and Music by Norman Whitfield and Barrett Strong

* Key signature denotes B♭ Dorian

** Includes Gtrs. 2 & 3

play 9 times

Gtrs. 2 & 3: w/ Riff A, till fade

Gtr. 1 tacet

1. It was the third of Septem-

* + = closed (toe down) o = open (toe up)

Verse
B♭m
Rhy. Fig. 1
End Rhy. Fig. 1
Gtr. 1
mp
ber. That day I'll al-ways re-mem - ber, yes I will, 'cause
Gtr. 4 (clean)
mf
hold bend
Gtr. 1: w/ Rhy. Fig. 1, 2 1/2 times
that was the day that my dad - dy died,
Gtr. 4
I nev - er got a chance to see him. Nev -
er heard noth-in' but bad things a - bout him. Ma - ma, I'm de - pend - ing on you
w/ pick & finger

lone. ___
('Lone.)

Oh, ___ Pa - pa was a roll - in' stone,

___ my ___ son, ___ yeah.

Wher - ev - er he laid his hat was his home. ___ (And

when he died,___) all ___ he ___ left us was a - lone." ___
('Lone.)

Well,___ well.

Gtr. 1

w/ wah-wah

Trumpet Solo
B♭m

Rhy. Fig. 2

Gtr. 1: w/ Rhy. Fig. 2, 3 times, simile
B♭m

End Rhy. Fig. 2

play 3 times

Interlude

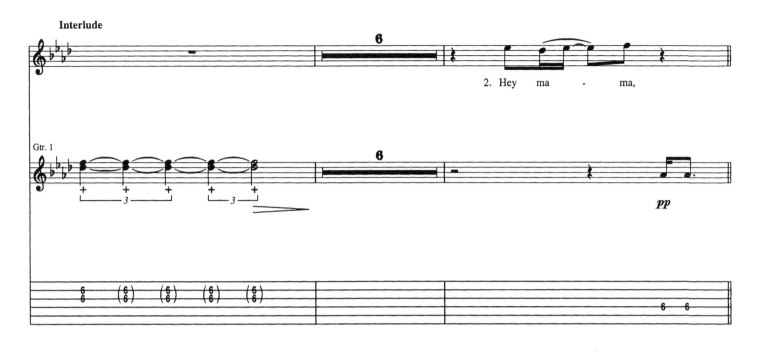

2. Hey ma - ma,

Verse

is it true what they say, that Pa - pa nev - er worked a day in his life?

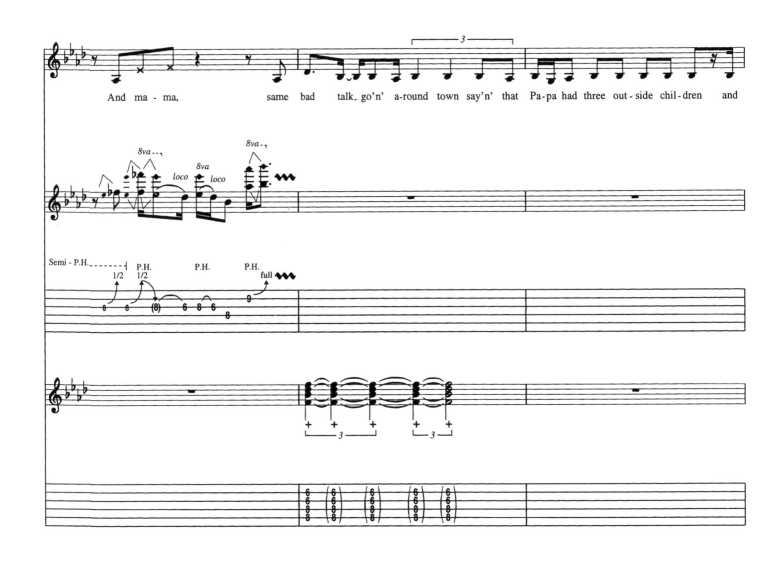

And ma - ma, same bad talk go'n' a-round town say'n' that Pa-pa had three out - side chil - dren and

a - noth - er wife, _ and that ain't right. Heard some talk a-bout Pa-pa do-in'

some store-front preach - in', talk-in' a-bout sav-in' souls, _ and all _ the time _ leach - in'. Deal -

Gtr. 4 tacet

- in' in dirt and steal - in' in the name of the Lord. _ Ma - ma just hung her head and said, "Pop;

Gtr. 1

*Open and close wah-wah rapidly while trem. picking

Chorus

Gtr. 3: w/ Fill 1, 2nd time; w/ Rhy. Fig. 3, 4 times, simile, 3rd time
Gtr. 4: w/ Riff B, 8 times
Bkgd. Voc.: w/ Voc. Fig. 1, 2 times

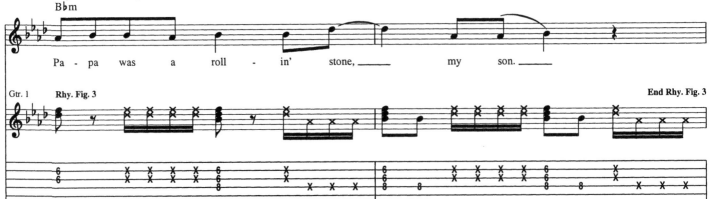

Pa - pa was a roll - in' stone, ____ my son. ____

Gtr. 1   Rhy. Fig. 3   End Rhy. Fig. 3

Wher - ev - er he laid his hat   was his home. ____   And

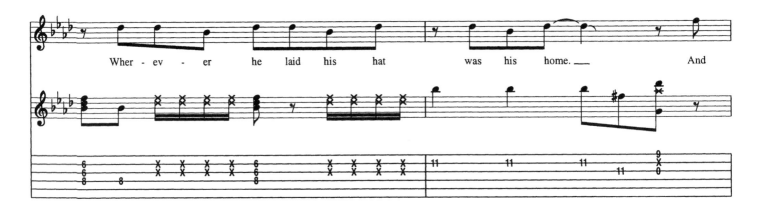

Riff B
Gtr. 4

Fill 1
Gtr. 1

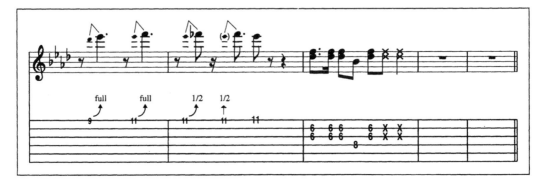

full   full   1/2   1/2

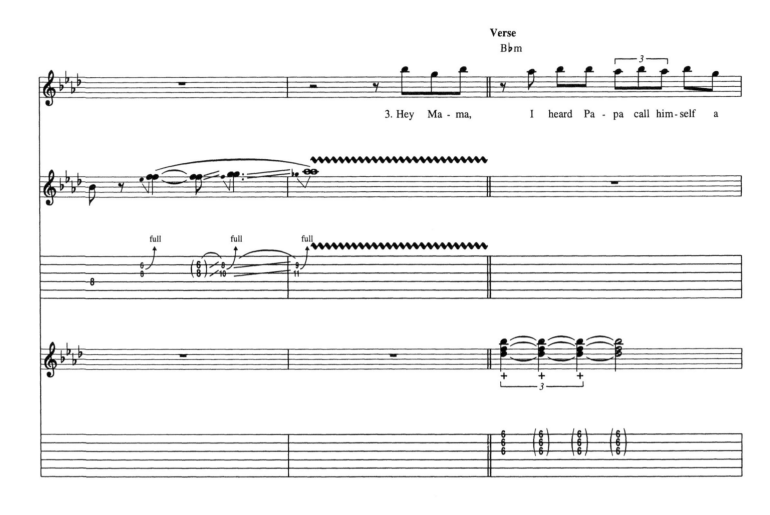

Verse

Bbm

3. Hey Ma - ma, I heard Pa - pa call him-self a

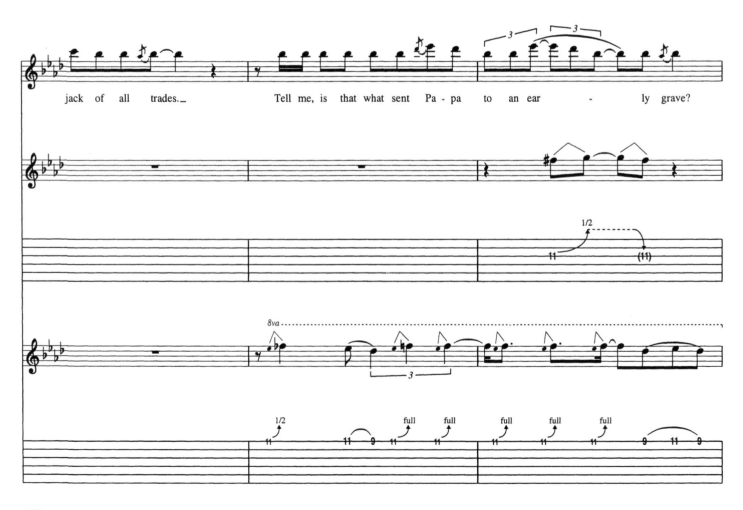

jack of all trades.___ Tell me, is that what sent Pa - pa to an ear - ly grave?

spent most of his time chas - in' wom - en and drink - in'. Ma - ma, I'm de - pend - in' on you

D.S. al Coda1

to tell me the truth. _____

Spoken: Mama looked up with a tear in her eye and said, "Son,...

full   full

⊕ *Coda1*

D.S. al Coda2

B♭m

lone _____ I said. _____
('Lone.)

⊕ *Coda2*

Play 4 Times and Fade

B♭m

Papa's Got a Brand New Bag

Words and Music by James Brown

*Chord symbols reflect implied tonality.

Pick Up the Pieces

Words and Music by James Hamish Stuart, Alan Gorrie, Roger Ball, Robbie McIntosh, Owen McIntyre and Malcolm Duncan

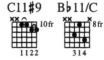

** Sax arr. for gtr.

* Chord symbols reflect overall harmony.

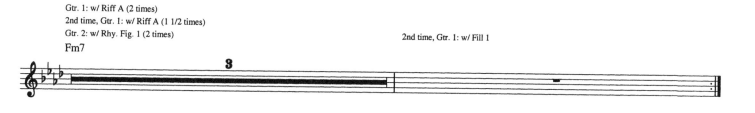

D.S. al Coda 1

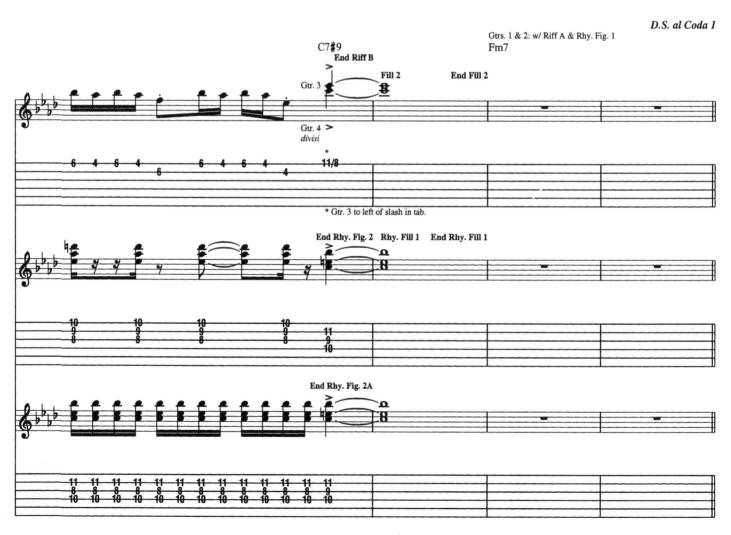

⊕ Coda 1

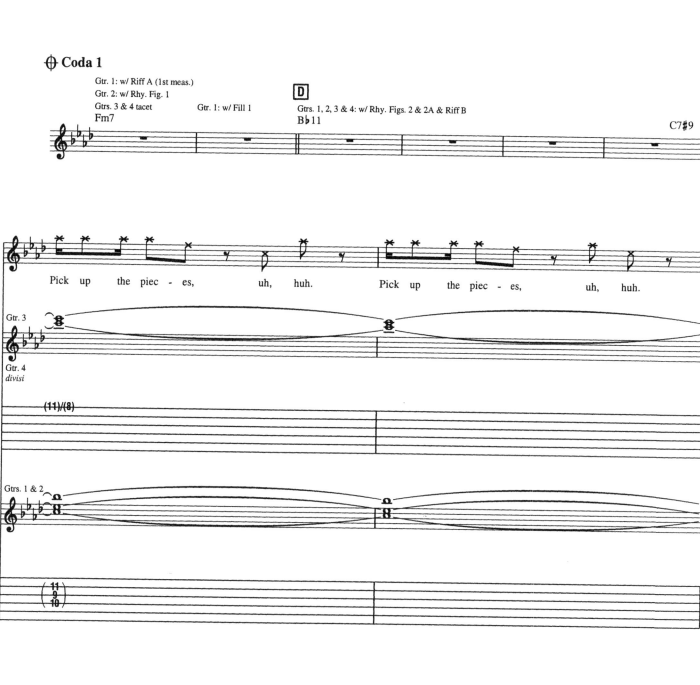

Please Accept My Love

Words and Music by B.B. King and Sam Ling

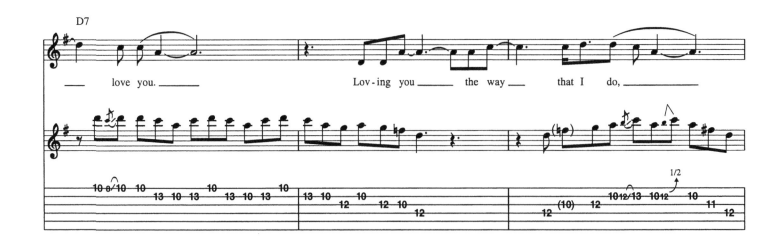

love you. Lov-ing you the way that I do,

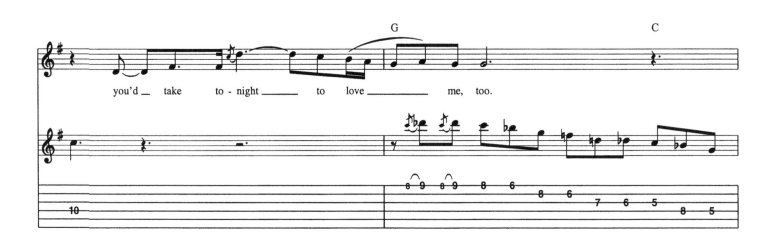

you'd take to-night to love me, too.

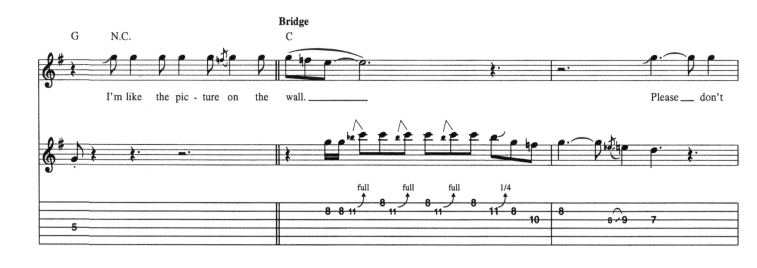

I'm like the pic-ture on the wall. Please don't

let me fall. It's my

I'll — end my life — to be — with you.   I'm like the pic-ture on —

Bridge

— the wall. —   Please _____ don't ___

— let — me fall. _____   It's my heart   I'm think-in' of. —

___   Won't you please,   please,   please — ac-cept my   love?   4. If you let   me be — your—

144

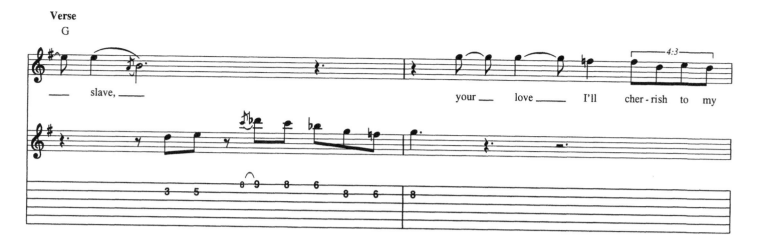

slave, _____ your ___ love _____ I'll cher-rish to my

grave. _____ And _ if you _ die be - fore _____ I do, _____

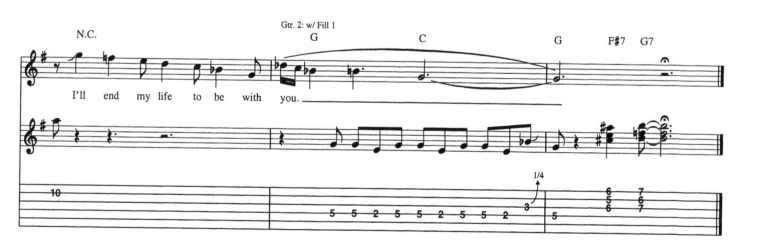

I'll end my life to be with you. _____

Fill 1
Gtr. 2 (clean)

Reach Out, I'll Be There

Words and Music by Brian Holland, Lamont Dozier and Edward Holland

hap-pi-ness _ is just an il - lu - sion, and your world _ a-round _ is crum-bl-ing _ down. _ Dar - ling. _

- sion, hap - pi - ness is just an il - lu - sion.

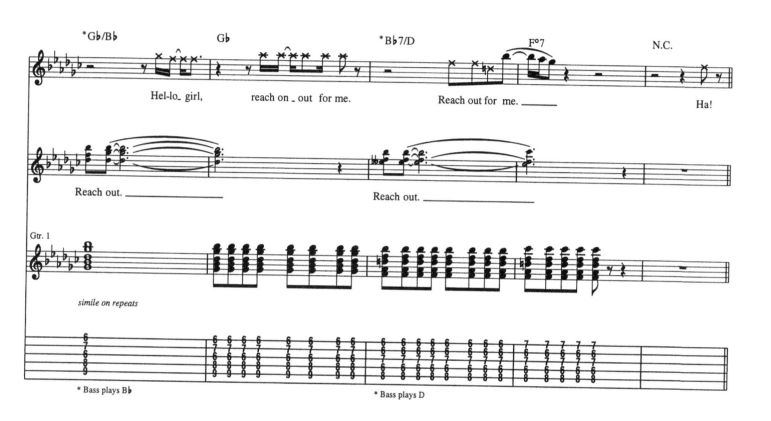

Hel-lo _ girl, reach on _ out for me. Reach out for me. _____ Ha!

Reach out. _____ Reach out. _____

Gtr. 1

simile on repeats

* Bass plays B♭   * Bass plays D

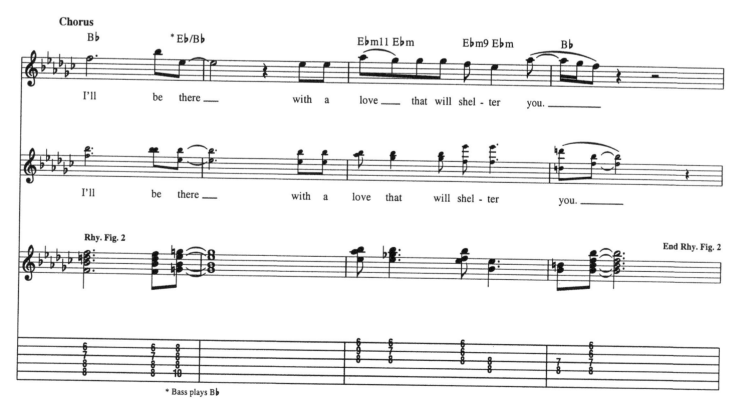

Chorus

I'll be there ___ with a love ___ that will shel - ter you. _____

I'll be there ___ with a love that will shel - ter you. _____

Rhy. Fig. 2   End Rhy. Fig. 2

* Bass plays B♭

Additional Lyrics

2. When you feel lost and about to give up,
   'Cause your best just ain't good enough.
   And you feel the world has grown cold,
   And you're drifting all on your own.
   And you need a hand to hold.
   Darlin', hello girl, reach out for me.
   Reach out for me.
   I'll be there to love and comfort you.
   And I'll be there to cherish and care for you...

3. I can the way you hang your head,
   You're without love now, now you're afraid.
   And through your tears you'll look around,
   But there's no peace of mind to be found.
   I know what you're thinkin': You're a loner, no love of your own.
   But darling, come on girl, reach out for me.
   Reach out. Just look over your shoulder.
   I'll be there to give you all the love you need.
   And I'll be there, you can always depend on me.

Rocket '88

Words and Music by Jackie Brenston

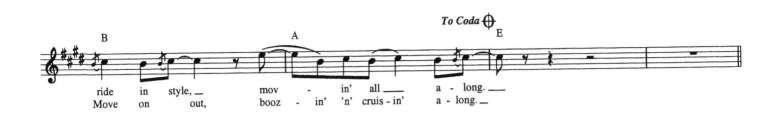

ride in style, ___ mov - in' all ___ a - long. ___
Move on out, booz - in' 'n' cruis - in' a - long. ___

Interlude

Gtr. 1: w/ Riff A
* Gtr. 2

* Tenor saxophones arr. for gtr.

Verse

Gtr. 1: w/ Riff A (1st 8 meas.)
Gtr. 2 tacet

2. V - eight mo - tor 'n' this smart ___ 'n' de - sign, black con - vert - a - ble top ___ an' the gals ___

___ don't ___ mind. ___ Sport - in' with me, ___ rid - in' all ___ 'round ___ town ___ for joy. ___

Sax Solo

Gtr. 1: w/ Rhy. Fig. 1 (3 times), simile

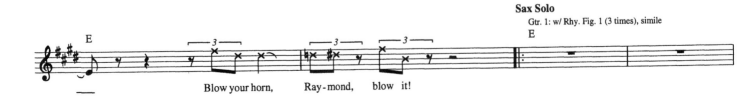

Blow your horn, Ray - mond, blow it!

Shining Star

Words and Music by Maurice White, Philip Bailey and Larry Dunn

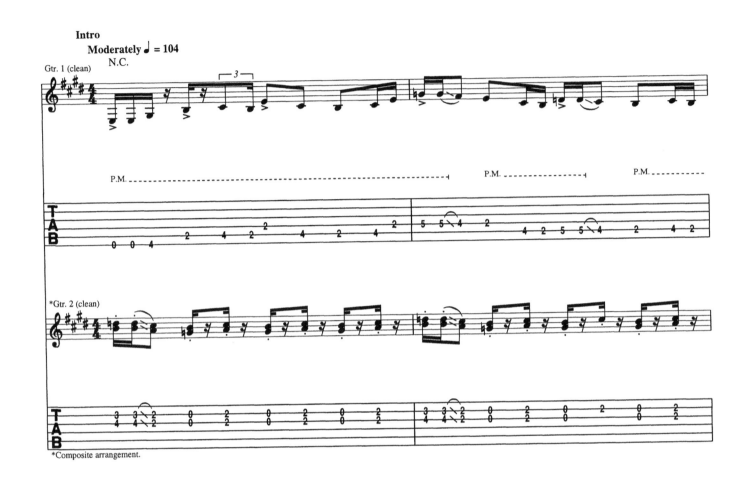

*Composite arrangement.

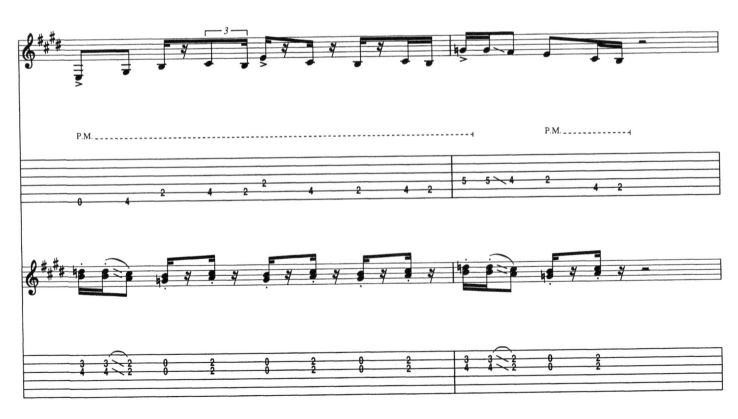

Yeah.

(Yeah, _____

Rhy. Fig. 1

End Rhy. Fig. 1

Gtr. 2: w/ Rhy. Fig. 1, simile

Hey. ____

Ha!

Gtr. 1

P.M. ----------- P.M. ----------- P.M. ----------- P.M. ----------- P.M. --

1/4

Verse

Gtr. 2: w/ Rhy. Fig. 1, 6 times, simile

E7#9

1. When you wish __ up - on __ a star, ____

your

sim.

1/4

1/4

*next 12 meas.

dreams will take＿ you ver‐y far,＿＿ yeah.＿＿ When＿

＿ you wish＿ up‐on＿ a dream,＿＿ life＿

＿ ain't al‐ways what＿ it seems,＿ oh, yeah.＿ What'd＿

＿ you see＿ on nights＿ of clear?＿＿ Hey.＿＿ In＿

the sky __ so ver - y dear, ___ yeah. ___

You're a

Chorus

Gtr. 2 tacet

N.C.(A7)   (D7)   (G7)   (C7)   (B7)

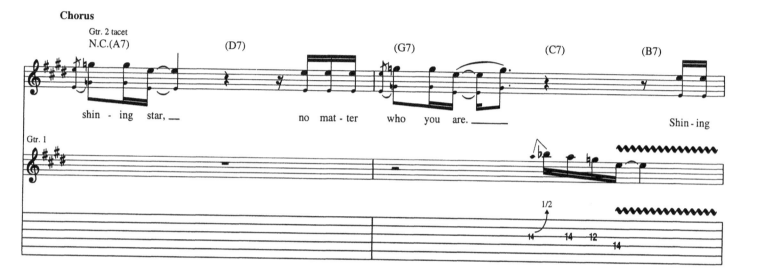

shin - ing star, __ no mat - ter who you are. ___

Shin - ing

Gtr. 1

(A7)   (D7)   (G7)   (C7)

bright to see ___ what you could tru - ly be, __ what you could tru - ly be. ___

Interlude

(Em)

Guitar Solo

(G7)   (G#7)   (A7)

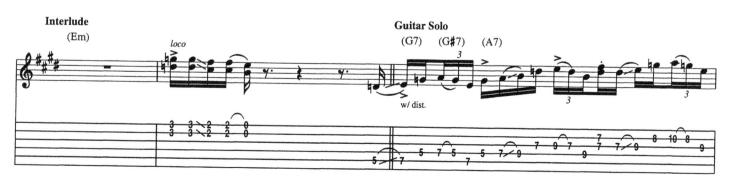

loco

w/ dist.

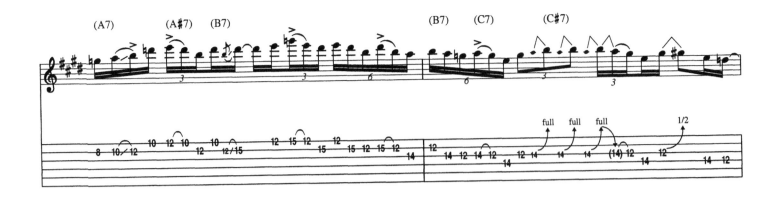

(A7) (A♯7) (B7) (B7) (C7) (C♯7)

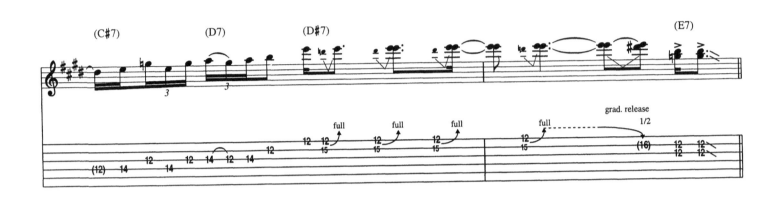

(C♯7) (D7) (D♯7) (E7)

Verse

Gtr. 2: w/ Rhy. Fig. 1, 12 times, simile

(E7♯9)

2. Shin-ing   star _ comes   in - to   view, ___

Gtr. 1

w/ clean tone   *sim.*

P.M. ------| P.M. ------------| P.M.---|

*next 23 meas.

shine his   watch - ful   light _ on   you. ___   Yeah. ___   Give

Shot Gun

Words and Music by Autry DeWalt

Ab

Intro

Saxophone Solo

* Key Signature denotes Ab Mixolydian.

%️ Chorus

**Organ arr. for gtr.

Sir Duke

Words and Music by Stevie Wonder

D.S. al Coda
End Riff A

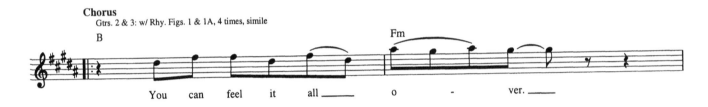

⊕ *Coda*

Chorus
Gtrs. 2 & 3: w/ Rhy. Figs. 1 & 1A, 4 times, simile

B

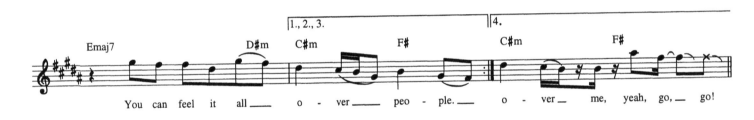

You can feel it all ____ o - ver. ____

You can feel it all ____ o - ver ____ peo - ple. ____ o - ver ____ me, yeah, go, ____ go!

Interlude
Gtr. 2: w/ Riff A

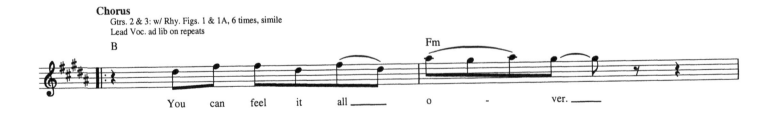

Chorus
Gtrs. 2 & 3: w/ Rhy. Figs. 1 & 1A, 6 times, simile
Lead Voc. ad lib on repeats

B

You can feel it all ____ o - ver. ____

Outro
Gtr. 2: w/ Riff A

You can feel it all ____ o - ver ____ peo - ple. ____ o - ver ____ peo - ple, go!

166

Super Freak

Words and Music by Rick James and Alonzo Miller

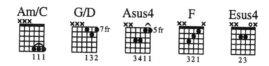

This Masquerade

Words and Music by Leon Russell

Are we real-ly hap-py here __ with this lone - ly game we play, __

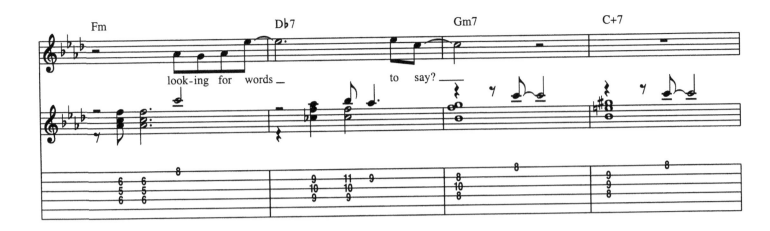

look-ing for words ___ to say?

Search-ing but not find - ing, un - der - stand - ing an - y - way; ___ we're

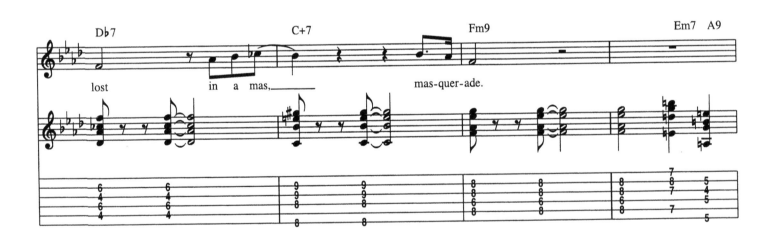

lost in a mas, ___ mas-quer-ade.

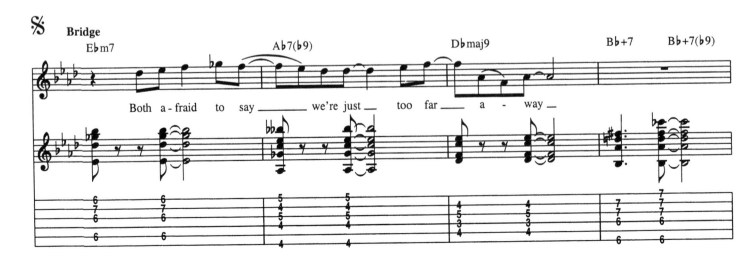

Bridge

Both a - fraid to say ___ we're just ___ too far ___ a - way ___

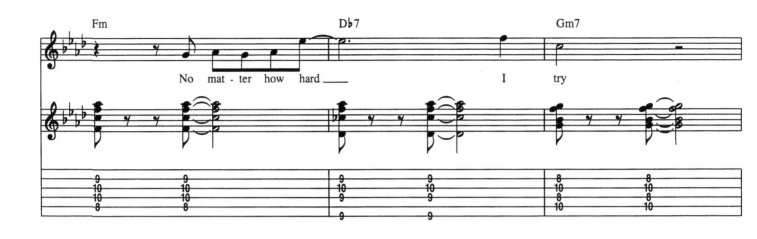

No mat - ter how hard ____ I try

to un - der - stand the rea - sons that we

To Coda ⊕

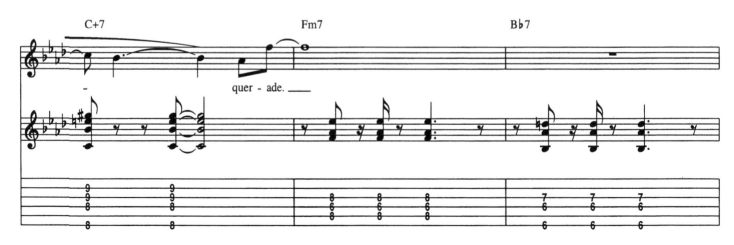

car - ry on ____ this way, ____ we're lost ____ in the mas-

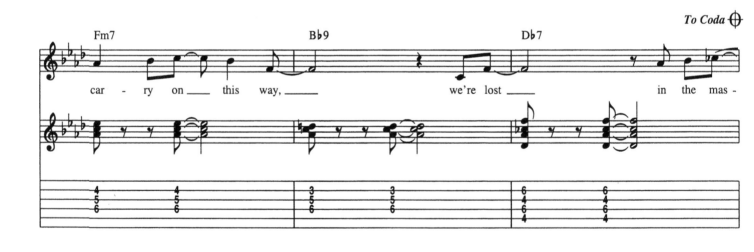

quer - ade. ____

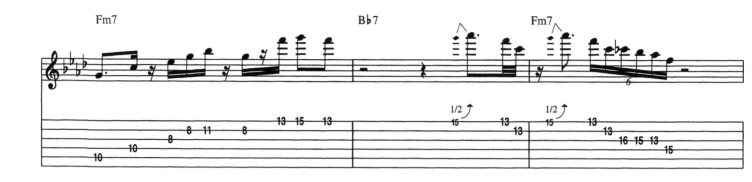

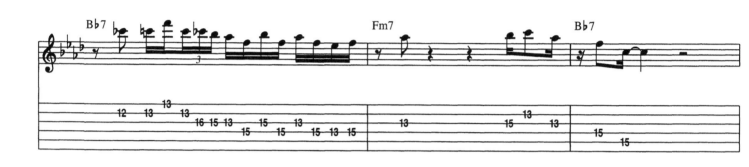

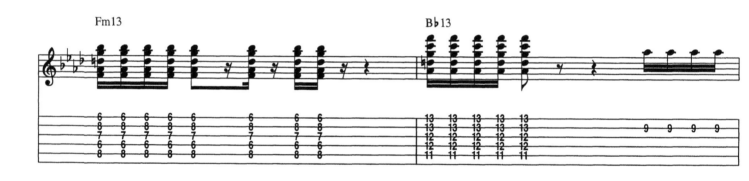

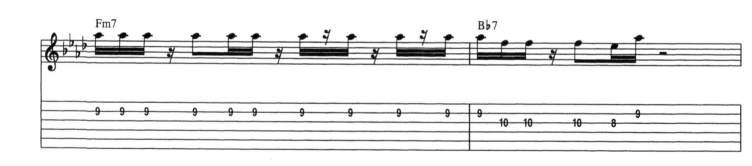

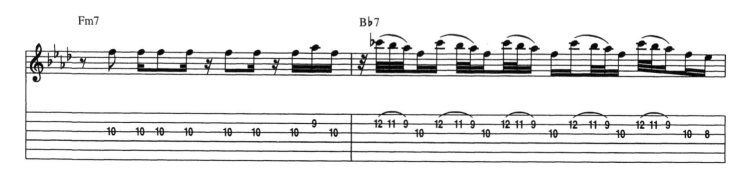

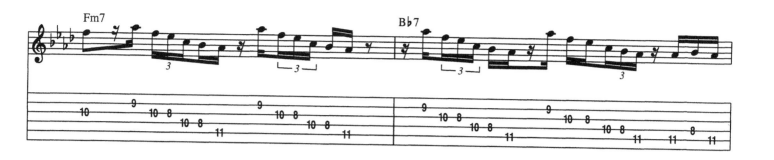

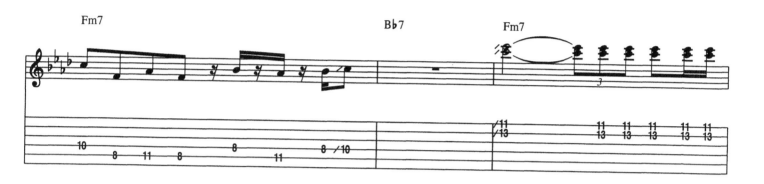

D. S. al Coda

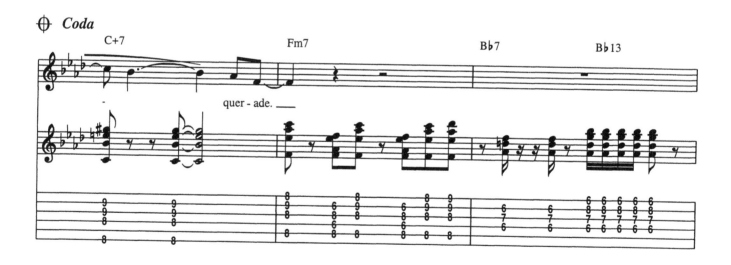

🞉 *Coda*

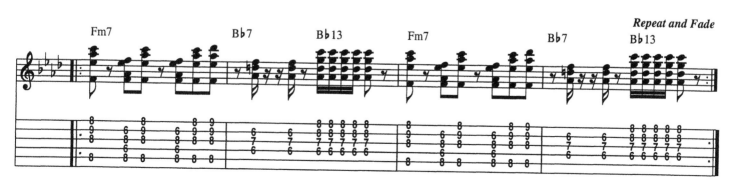

177

You've Really Got a Hold on Me

Words and Music by William "Smokey" Robinson

(Your Love Keeps Lifting Me) Higher and Higher

Words and Music by Gary Jackson, Carl Smith and Raynard Miner

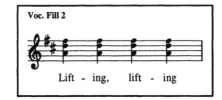

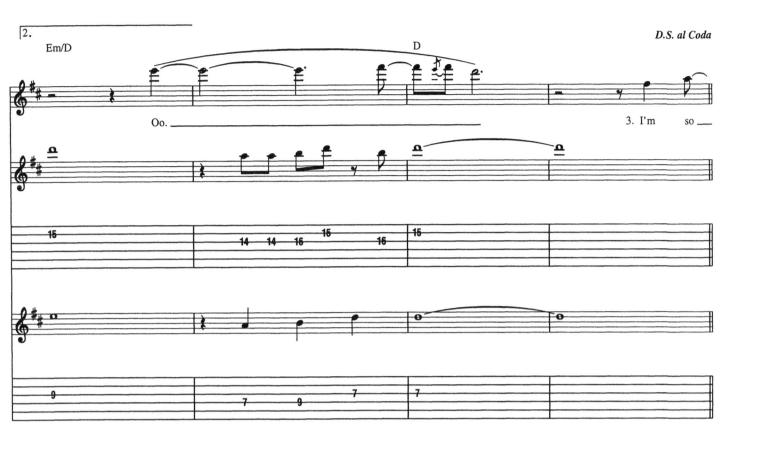

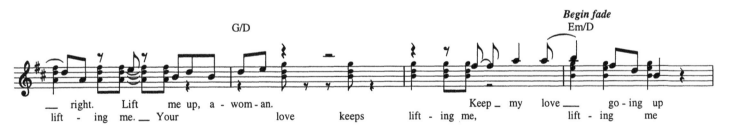

Guitar Notation Legend

Guitar Music can be notated three different ways: on a *musical staff*, in *tablature*, and in *rhythm slashes*.

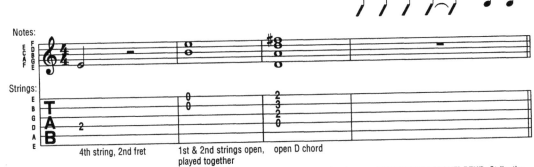

RHYTHM SLASHES are written above the staff. Strum chords in the rhythm indicated. Use the chord diagrams found at the top of the first page of the transcription for the appropriate chord voicings. Round noteheads indicate single notes.

THE MUSICAL STAFF shows pitches and rhythms and is divided by bar lines into measures. Pitches are named after the first seven letters of the alphabet.

TABLATURE graphically represents the guitar fingerboard. Each horizontal line represents a string, and each number represents a fret.

4th string, 2nd fret   1st & 2nd strings open, played together   open D chord

HALF-STEP BEND: Strike the note and bend up 1/2 step.

WHOLE-STEP BEND: Strike the note and bend up one step.

GRACE NOTE BEND: Strike the note and bend up as indicated. The first note does not take up any time.

SLIGHT (MICROTONE) BEND: Strike the note and bend up 1/4 step.

BEND AND RELEASE: Strike the note and bend up as indicated, then release back to the original note. Only the first note is struck.

PRE-BEND: Bend the note as indicated, then strike it.

VIBRATO: The string is vibrated by rapidly bending and releasing the note with the fretting hand.

WIDE VIBRATO: The pitch is varied to a greater degree by vibrating with the fretting hand.

HAMMER-ON: Strike the first (lower) note with one finger, then sound the higher note (on the same string) with another finger by fretting it without picking.

PULL-OFF: Place both fingers on the notes to be sounded. Strike the first note and without picking, pull the finger off to sound the second (lower) note.

LEGATO SLIDE: Strike the first note and then slide the same fret-hand finger up or down to the second note. The second note is not struck.

SHIFT SLIDE: Same as legato slide, except the second note is struck.

TRILL: Very rapidly alternate between the notes indicated by continuously hammering on and pulling off.

TAPPING: Hammer ("tap") the fret indicated with the pick-hand index or middle finger and pull off to the note fretted by the fret hand.

NATURAL HARMONIC: Strike the note while the fret-hand lightly touches the string directly over the fret indicated.

PINCH HARMONIC: The note is fretted normally and a harmonic is produced by adding the edge of the thumb or the tip of the index finger of the pick hand to the normal pick attack.

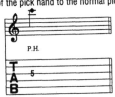

PICK SCRAPE: The edge of the pick is rubbed down (or up) the string, producing a scratchy sound.

MUFFLED STRINGS: A percussive sound is produced by laying the fret hand across the string(s) without depressing, and striking them with the pick hand.

PALM MUTING: The note is partially muted by the pick hand lightly touching the string(s) just before the bridge.

RAKE: Drag the pick across the strings indicated with a single motion.

TREMOLO PICKING: The note is picked as rapidly and continuously as possible.

VIBRATO BAR DIVE AND RETURN: The pitch of the note or chord is dropped a specified number of steps (in rhythm) then returned to the original pitch.

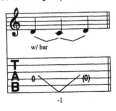

VIBRATO BAR SCOOP: Depress the bar just before striking the note, then quickly release the bar.

VIBRATO BAR DIP: Strike the note and then immediately drop a specified number of steps, then release back to the original pitch.

184